ALMA DE GROEN was born in New Zealand in 1941. In 1964 she settled in Australia where, under the influence of the new theatre movement, she began writing plays in 1968. Between 1969 and 1972 she spent four years overseas among artists in England, France and Canada. In 1970 she won a Canadian national playwriting competition with her short work, *The Joss Adams Show*, which received a workshop performance by the Shakespearean Festival Theatre, Stratford, Ontario, and a reading at the Studio Laboratory Theatre, Toronto. It has since been performed in most Australian capital cities as well as in London.

Her first full-length play, *The Sweatproof Boy* (later shortened into *Perfectly All Right*), was presented at Nimrod Street Theatre in 1972. *The After-Life of Arthur Cravan* was selected for the inaugural Australian National Playwrights' Conference in 1973 and a season followed at Sydney's Jane Street Theatre. *Going Home* (1976) and *Chidley* (1977), both premiered in Melbourne. *Vocations*, workshopped by the ANPC in 1981, opened at Melbourne Theatre Company the next year.

Alma was awarded the 1985 Australian Writers Guild AWGIE Award for her television adaptation of Glen Tomasetti's novel, *Man of Letters*. Following a 1986 ANPC workshop, *The Rivers of China* had its premiere at Sydney Theatre Company in 1987, winning the Premier's Literary Award for Drama in both New South Wales and Victoria. *The Girl Who Saw Everything* opened at Melbourne's Russell Street Theatre in 1991 and later won an AWGIE Award for Best Stage Play. In 1998 it was performed at the Drama Theatre in Ho Chi Minh City.

Her writing for radio includes *Available Light* and *Stories in the Dark* (with Ian Mackenzie), which was the Australian 1996 Prix Italia entry. In November 1998, Alma became the first playwright to receive the Patrick White Literary Award.

Julia Blake as Anna Akhmatova in the 1998 Melbourne Theatre Company production. (Photo: Jeff Busby)

The WOMAN *in the* WINDOW

Alma De Groen

Currency Press • Sydney

CURRENCY PLAYS

First published in 1999
by Currency Press Pty Ltd,
PO Box 2287, Strawberry Hills, NSW, 2012, Australia
enquiries@currency.com.au
www.currency.com.au

Reprinted 2012, 2019

NATIONAL LIBRARY OF AUSTRALIA CIP DATA

    De Groen, Alma, 1941–.
    The woman in the window.
    ISBN 9780868195933 (pbk.)
    I. Title.
A822.3

Publication of this title was assisted by the Commonwealth
Government through the Australia Council, its arts funding and
advisory body.

Contents

Typeset by Erin Dewar for Currency Press.
Printed by Fineline Print & Copy Service, St Peters, NSW.
Cover design by Trevor Hood, Anaconda Graphics
Cover photograph shows Sophie Gregg (left), Paul English (centre) and Julia
Blake in the 1998 Melbourne Theatre Company production. (Photo: Jeff Busby)

Sophie Gregg as Rachel in the 1998 Melbourne Theatre Company production. (Photo: Jeff Busby)

The Play and Its Plot

Elizabeth Perkins

The Woman in the Window is named for the Russian poet Anna Akhmatova (1889–1966) who was kept under surveillance in Stalinist Russia for long periods between 1934 and 1956. For many Russians the inspiring poems she wrote during the terrible war years from 1940 to 1945 gave expression to their own grief and pain and helped them to fight and survive in the trenches or in besieged cities like Leningrad. After 1946, it was alleged her work was too remote from the concerns of socialist reconstruction, and she was forbidden to write her own poetry and allowed only to translate poetry approved by Stalin. She was also required to show herself to Russian police by standing at her window twice a day. What the Russian Government really feared was the proven power of her writing, which might strengthen the people now suffering a new pain and terror under the Stalinist regime. Alma De Groen's work often refers directly and indirectly to the power of great art to subvert the coercive and destructive forces that exercise control in a society.

The Woman in the Window pursues this idea in both time-frames in which the drama takes place. Akhmatova, known to some as a shaman in her lifetime, is shown communicating in spirit with the young woman Rachel, who is trapped in the monstrous super-society of 2300. The state is no longer a political state. All national assets have been sold off to private enterprise which has become one huge monopolist business corporation controlled by totalitarian politics and made possible by the perverted use of technology. The glimpse of the future is set in Australia. The emprisoned society of Stalinist Russia is magnified and made even more terrible in the underground cities created by a technology that controls all facets of life. A hierarchical structure exists made up of those considered essential to manipulate a technological society, and others, like artists, poets, musicians, technicians and women 'servicers' of all kinds who may at any time be disposed of.

As in De Groen's *The Rivers of China*, the dramaturgy weaves together the two interacting stories and time-frames. With several characters in each period involved in associated stories, the play is a rich texture of dramatic action. When every moment is given its own weight in the theatre, however, the lines of the drama are made clear and distinct. The meaning of each smaller piece of action reinforces the others, and contributes to the overall significance of the play.

To achieve this richness but also preserve immediate dramatic intelligibility, De Groen has used easily recognised tropes or situations to present this challenging vision of the past and the future, with its implicit warning and final steadfast hope. Each of these readily identified situations, however, has a new aspect or dramatic twist.

The desperate plight of individuals in Stalinist Moscow is depicted through the friendship between Akhmatova and the discredited mathematics teacher Lilli; and by the spying of their terrified neighbour Tusya, who nevertheless loses her scientist husband when he rashly criticises the irresponsible disposal of nuclear waste. The companionship between the mystical, impractical, visionary Akhmatova and the practical, ironic mathematician Lilli, has a new dimension, because Lilli is memorising Anna's poems as she composes them. As the poet's apartment was searched for forbidden writing, Akhmatova's friends did, in real life, preserve her poems by committing them to memory. After the death of her husband, Tusya feels that she has little more to lose, and instead of spying on Akhmatova for the MGB, she is seen in the later scenes taking up Lilli's task of memorising Akhmatova's poems.

The two MGB officers, the urban Korzh and the country-boy Stetsky, reconstruct the menace and bleak humour associated with terrorist regimes, but the familiar interrogation scenes, the last leading to Lilli's death, retain their power to evoke revulsion at destructive stupidity, cunning and brutality.

The oppressive, claustrophobic world of 2300 suffers from a much more powerful and intrusive surveillance than anything the MGB could impose. This world becomes intelligible to the audience as they follow the stories of the two Conference Stress Consultants, Rachel and Maren, their female supervisor Miz, and Rachel's client, the registered poet Sandor. Although Maren is fortunate to be one of the five per cent of the inhabitants of this super-state who have employment (the remainder apparently sedated by addictive goggling-in to the virtual reality of their computers), she takes her own life when she realises that a past client, a musician, has disappeared, been deleted, de-listed, along with other musicians, because computers are better than people at composing music. A file in the computer bank is the only guarantee and record of existence. If some citizens today cling to the belief 'I have a birth certificate, tax file or pension card number, therefore I exist', the prospect in 2300 is even bleaker. Maren leaves to her friend Rachel her virtual reality room which she has constructed to represent the night sky, seen in nature only by the very privileged elite in this society.

The friendship of Akhmatova and Lilli is the warm personal strand in the earlier time-frame; the love and shared quest between Rachel and Sandor humanises the future world and leads the audience forward. The quest undertaken by Rachel and Sandor is to recover from the computer archives the poetry of past generations because poetry has been declared economically unviable and all poems and poets are threatened with permanent de-listing. Material regarded as conferring power, or as subversive to the corporation, is in deep storage or, if considered irrelevant, is simply deleted from the data base. As in Stalin's Russia, economic rationalism prevails, and people or professions that are not seen as contributing directly to the economy are, in fact, regarded as subversive of the corporation enterprise. There is constant surveillance of access to the hierarchical archives, and Rachel and Sandor are in danger of detection and punishment.

Women poets have long since disappeared from the accessible archives, but urged by Akhmatova's watching spirit, Rachel taps deeper and deeper into the archives, downloading to her own computer space female as well as male writers. So Rachel goes even further than Sandor wants: the deeper she goes, the greater the chance of detection. Sandor's and Rachel's researches are detected and Sandor is disposed of but not before he protects all the poetry from permanent destruction by creating the tardigrade virus.

Some of the essential elements of *The Woman in the Window* that should emerge in a stage production are the similarities between any twentieth-century totalitarian regime and the future super-society governed by economic rationalism and industrial mega-corporations. The ever-present Korzh and Stetsky and the clumsy listening devices in Akhmatova's ceiling are forebears of the apparently impossible technology for spying on an individual's physical, mental and emotional movements. Miz and the Auditor, the visible manifestations of this surveillance, have more sophisticated devices for interrogation and detection, but the rivalry between them, and the Auditor's exploitation of power are found in every corrupt state. Under Stalin's regime, artists and their work also disappeared although their disposal may not have been as simple as in the super-state. The real-life stratagem by which Akhmatova's friends memorised and preserved her poems is reflected in Sandor's use of the tardigrade virus which, like the organism after which he names it, can lie dormant for at least a hundred years under all conditions, and can re-activate itself at any time.

Another facet of *The Woman in the Window* that should be clear is that the play does not set up an opposition between the human imagination and scientific reasoning, and it does not criticise the technological developments that still give concern to many at the end of the twentieth century. Preservation of Akhmatova's poems depended on the resources of human memory. Preservation of the world heritage of poetry depended on Sandor's imaginative and technical skill in creating the tardigrade virus that guarded essential parts of the archival memory of the computer.

The tardigrade is a 'water bear animalcule' visible under magnification, which is given to Rachel by a former client, a biologist, who told her that she should have it because 'It's an animal that can switch life on and off'. The tardigrade images the human spirit and creative energy which can lie dormant for long periods under oppression, and come to life again with renewed strength. The tardigrade does exist. The technology used in the play, which some may find presently incredible, either exists or is foreseeably probable. A helpful program could supply brief notes on some of these matters of fact, like the computerisation of books and their deletion from accessible records, but as concepts such as 'Smart Rooms' and the completely digital library are rapidly becoming household words, notes may soon be unnecessary.

The element of the play that may concern those who can happily accept the apparently science-fiction world of technology, is the world of the spirit that enables Akhmatova to converse with long-dead poets, and with Lilli after her friend's death, and to foresee Rachel's world and to communicate ideas to the girl. This may be seen also as the possibility of the mind, spirit and physical body moving through time and space, and as a simple extension of the idea of the relativity of time and space. To others in the audience, one of the most credible aspects of the play will be the ability to be inspired and led by those who lived before us, and the ability of certain people, like shamans and other spiritual leaders, to foresee future events. The poetry of even the most respectable of English poets, like Alfred Lord Tennyson, and the Irish poet W.B. Yeats, has examples of this kind of foreseeing.

The Woman in the Window celebrates the endurance of the human spirit of creativity. It is also a warning, a kind of foreseeing like that given by W.B. Yeats when he wrote the poem called 'The Second Coming'. Akhmatova is certainly a victim of the totalitarian regime that followed the Russian Revolution. She realises that she and her generation of young, intellectual, liberated Russian writers who celebrated life so hugely at the beginning of the twentieth century were also partly responsible, because of their complacency, for the conditions that made the Revolution possible. 'We danced and made love on the edge of an inferno. We tumbled into Terror in our Carnival masks and our satin shoes. There were people starving, who had no shelter, who couldn't read, and we didn't care.' The warning, the 'awful lesson' in De Groen's play, is not so much about class and social justice, although that is part of it, as against a new *fin-de-siècle* complacency about selling off the natural world and everything a nation owns to giant corporations in exchange for—what?

The play seems to suggest that some real advance in human stature would be achieved if only technology could work with this human spirit that lies outside the understanding of even the most advanced technology. With Ian Mackenzie, who is a computer analyst and writer, De Groen keeps abreast of scientific and technological developments, and interprets these advances in terms of human values. De Groen herself obviously has no difficulty in seeing the two great forces of intellect and spirit joining with the human imagination, not only to create visions of better futures, but also eventually to bring them about.

De Groen's plays do not usually display the snapping, one-liner wit that audience's love in the work of some Australian playwrights, but even her scenes with the most serious import often carry an ironic, sometimes tender and sometimes dry humour. A production will be alert to the importance of allowing each of these moments to have their own allotted space. De Groen's script creates these brief moments with theatrical tact and dramatic awareness of the way they can heighten the emotional and intellectual experience for the audience.

Good drama does not provide answers or happy endings: but the greatest drama always offers hope. At the first reading of *The Woman in the Window* at the National Playwrights' Conference in 1997, the only dry eyes around the table as the run-through ended were those of the playwright and Ian. Tentative and interrupted as the reading was, with the actors and director reading the script together for the first time, the power of the play and its theme overwhelmed all of us. It was not because *The Woman in the Window* is sad in the conventional sense or because its vision of the future is bleak. Indeed it is not. The lines from Ahkmatova's poem, 'The Muse', written in 1931, with which the poet ends the play, are deeply moving of course. But since they have the same effect when spoken in Russian, English, French or German, for example, it is not the poetry only that silences us at the end of De Groen's play. The movement of the drama through scenes which enact the denial and the affirmation of human freedom and courage, leads to a final assertion of the indestructibility of the creative imagination and of life itself. The energy of spirit that dictated to the thirteenth-century poet Dante his vision of Hell in *The Inferno*, has accompanied us down the centuries and will come with us into whatever technological heaven or hell we may devise for ourselves in the future. It is the hope in De Groen's play that moves us to tears.

Elizabeth Perkins

Elizabeth Perkins was the dramaturg for the workshopping of *The Woman in the Window* at the Australian National Playwrights' Conference, Canberra, in 1997. She is an Associate Professor at James Cook University and has written *The Plays of Alma De Groen* (Amsterdam: Rodopi, 1994).

Notes on a Hypothetical Future

Ian Mackenzie

The Woman in the Window is set partly in the Cold War period of the 1950s and partly in the 23rd Century. The past scenes examine what history tells us about the damage caused to society by a government which rules by fear, and oppresses the creative spirit. The future scenes imagine what life could be like if we allow technology to displace art, literature and the natural world.

The culture that exists in this fictional 23rd Century is what is left after a rather Darwinian survival of the technologically literate. Society has ended up like this because individuals exercised cumulative apathy ('She'll be right, mate') while the groups that actually worked to shape the future shaped it to their own advantage. 'Knowledge itself is power', said Francis Bacon, but this is the world of information. If art and literature are thought too insignificant to digitise, or if it is easier to keep people amused with addictive computer games (a 23rd-century interactive virtual reality known as 'Ractives'), then their loss goes unremarked.

This is a world governed by the ideological descendants of today's managers, economists, and politicians—a tiny elite who want to arrange life for their own benefit, and to deliver the minimum of services with the absolute minimum of workers. The engineering challenges of the world have by this time all been solved. Everyone has food, drink, shelter and other material comforts; and as much Ractive as they want. No pressure has been placed on them to downsize the populace; in fact, they have been encouraged to increase their numbers until the entire useable surface of the Earth has become living space.

Now the whole environment is artificial—rooms, corridors, ceilings, floors. It is many generations since common people saw the outside world or the sky as a matter of course. They live in a single windowless apartment building/arcology that has spread over the entire planet. On its 'roof', i.e. the new surface of the Earth, there are greenhouses full of algae absorbing and utilising the sunlight to feed the populace and generate oxygen. The food supply is uniform and comes from the equivalent of a planetary-sized 'Biosphere 3'. Everything is recycled, everything is produced 'efficiently' with no wasteful food chain between the photosynthetic algae and the consumer. Their water supply is endlessly recycled from their sewage, like their food.

Rachel's job is prized because it is seen to have meaning. People who don't have jobs spend their time plugged into Ractives. A tracer functions as a map, an electronic diary, a wristwatch, an identity badge, a mobile phone...

Here are some other terms and concepts the play utilises. A launch analyst is someone who oversees rocket launches and plans their trajectory. Mass drivers are an idea borrowed from science fiction—they bear a resemblance to a 'railgun' from the SDI (Strategic Defence Initiative, aka 'Star Wars') program, but are generally imagined as a large installation on the moon or on an asteroid, which uses electromagnetic propulsion to accelerate many tons of mass into orbit. They work best in a vacuum because anything travelling that fast in atmosphere will usually melt (and suffer immense aerodynamic drag).

When Lilli says: 'Our Great Leader could declare pi to be three' (p.6), she means that pi (π) is a transcendental number defined in mathematics as the ratio of a circle's circumference to its diameter. Its decimal places go on for infinity without repeating (the value is 3.1415926535...). A hexagon has six sides, of which each is one half of the 'diameter' connecting any two opposite vertices. Therefore, the circumference of a hexagon is exactly three times its diameter. So if pi was declared to be three, circles would have to be distorted into hexagons for this to be true.

Being 'goggled in' simply means putting on wrap-around display glasses and a headband (which is full of superconducting magnets and more computing power than the entire world has in 1999) to induce currents in the brain to give the sense of reality. It is a sinister extrapolation of existing media technology because it has learned how to addict the user by constantly adding subliminal elements to the Ractive and expanding on whatever captures the user's interest.

Flatland, by Edwin A. Abbott, a story about life on a surface such as a piece of paper, is one book which explores the two-dimensional world. Two more modern explorations are: *The Planiverse*, by A.K. Dewdney, and *Sphereland*, by Dionys Budrys.[1]

In our imaginary 23rd Century, bureaucratic inertia has allowed Earth's surroundings to become overloaded with space stations. With so much spoil from strip-mining the moon, it had seemed easy to form the spoil into space stations and launch them closer to Earth to become low-gravity playgrounds for the rulers. This not entirely a fiction: there is already talk of strip-mining the moon for fusion power. The moon has an isotope of helium—'Helium 3'—which could allow fusion power plants to run without producing radioactive by-products. Earth has lost almost all of its helium, so pollution-free fusion power is no longer obtainable.

Alma wanted the moon to appear half its present size. Initially, I wondered if the moon could be literally half the size because $\frac{7}{8}$ $(1-(\frac{1}{2})3)$ of it had been turned into space stations. The calculations demonstrated that about 68 billion space stations would need to be built to have this result. Also, the technology (and cumulative effort) to significantly change the visible size of the moon needed a few hundred years to develop and run.

So we had to find another reason. What if the moon were approximately its present size, but twice as far away? The energy to push it this far out would come from the gravitational energy gained by launching vast numbers of space stations into lower orbits than that of the moon's present orbit (averaging 3,600 kilometres above the Earth's surface compared with 384,400). In this case, only a feasible 100 million space stations would be needed to make the moon appear half its present size. A lunar month would then be about 79 days.

To reach these numbers, I turned to the concept of self-replicating machines. Suppose, for the sake of argument, in ten or twenty years' time, we launch some very special autonomous robots onto the moon's surface. These robots use only materials available on the moon. They take ten years to build a factory and a launcher (mass driver if you

1   Edwin A. Abbott, *Flatland*, 1884; A.K. Dewdney, *The Planiverse Computer Contact with a Two-Dimensional World*, New York: Posiedon/Simon & Schuster, 1984; Dionys Budrys, *Sphereland*, Oxford: BasilBlackwell, 1963.

prefer). Each factory takes another ten years to build not only another set of robots, but a space station which is launched into orbit around the Earth. Once the robots or factories finish their task, they start again. The number of robots, factories and space stations follow an exponential growth, doubling every ten years, and exceeding 100 million after 28 doublings.

From a space station, one's experience of the horizon is different from that on Earth.. Inhabitants of a space station live on the inside of a cylinder: as they look at the distant landscape, it curves up over their heads and behind them. These cylinders are rotating, so as to give a sense of gravity through centrifugal (centripetal if you're a physicist) force.

A 'preservation' is part nature preserve on Earth and part illusion. The experience of distance is provided by an artificially-created sense of perspective in which things more than a couple of hundred metres away are scaled down so that by, say, five hundred metres from the centre there are bonsai pines on foot-high 'mountains'. When we see Rachel and Sandor in the virtual room, we see their virtual selves. Virtuality here has advanced to the point where not only does it seem real, but anyone can create their own reality.

It is in this artificial world that the characters in *The Woman in the Window* face the issue of the value of history. The archives' systems are outdated; they are bulky and slow compared to 2300 technology. They could be converted to the new technology but no one has an answer to the question 'why bother?' Few people access the archives and they are using up valuable space and materials. The authorities vote to discard them in the name of 'efficiency'.

Rachel is able to talk to her computer because speech recognition is an accepted fact; and she has grown up with a computer sub-routine (a computer nanny) which has been her companion since birth. The laws of physics might even provide an explanation of how Akhmatova and Rachel can communicate. Lilli refers to our living in Einstein's four-dimensional space-time, which could (if seen from some higher dimensional space) be curved, twisted, even passing through a part of itself at an earlier time. (Lilli would, of course, have been unaware of Hugh Everett's interpretation of quantum mechanics, *Many Worlds*, which was not published until 1957.[2]) The hypothesis is that when two times are passing through one another, there could be a subtle quantum interference between them, and that although most minds would not be equipped to handle information resulting from such a connection, the mind of a shaman such as Akhmatova might be able to see in it a glimpse of the future.

Ian Mackenzie
Science Advisor

---

2   Hugh C. Everett, '"Relative State" formulation of quantum mechanics' in J.A. Wheeler and W.H. Zurek, *Quantum Theory and Measurement*, Princeton University Press, 1983.

A child said *What is the grass?* Fetching it to me with full hands;
How could I answer the child? I do not know what it is any more
than he.

I guess it must be the flag of my disposition, out of hopeful green
stuff woven.

From *Song of Myself. A Child Said What is the Grass?*
Walt Whitman

ACKNOWLEDGMENTS

I want to thank the Australia Council, the Melbourne Theatre Company, the Sydney Theatre Company and the Australian National Playwrights' Centre whose support made *The Woman in the Window* possible.

I am indebted to numerous individuals in the play's development. Special thanks are due to:

May-Brit Akerholt, Artistic Director of the Playwrights' Conference, who took the play under her wing and provided encouragement and incentive to continue with it, and gave me Kate Cherry as its director at the 1997 conference; my friend Dr Elizabeth Perkins of James Cook University who dramaturged the play; the astute and supportive cast on that occasion: Julia Blake, Leah Purcell, Tyler Coppin, Dina Panozzo, Nicholas Hammond, Gillian Hyde, Pat Hutchinson, and the remarkable Peter Kingston, who stepped into the breach for a couple of days and briefly took over the role of Akhmatova!

My thanks to director Rodney Fisher for his inspirational enthusiasm, and the cast of the play's reading at the Sydney Theatre Company on 10 April 1997, who coped heroically with a script which was still many drafts from completion, and gave a sensitive and moving public reading after one day's rehearsal: Anna Volska, Essie Davis, Gosia Dobrowolska, Tara Morice, Andrew Rodereda, Tony Phelan and Helen Dallimore.

My thanks to Roger Hodgman, Peter Matheson and Bruce Myles at Melbourne Theatre Company for their support, and to the cast for their insights, suggestions and commitment to the play. The opportunity to work with them, and designers Richard Roberts, Anna French, Matt Scott and composer Andrew Pendlebury was a great joy to me.

It was a privilege to work with director Kate Cherry and be a part of her Melbourne Theatre Company debut. My thanks to Kate for many months of uniquely informative, rewarding and life-enhancing dramaturgy. Any playwright who gets to work with Kate gains a treasure.

Eureka Theatre Company allowed me to make a final fine-tune of the script. My thanks to director Camilla Blunden and the cast who triumphed over a freezing scout hall to provide a wealth of intelligent and creative encouragement.

Finally, my thanks to Ian Mackenzie to whom I turned for answers to the 'what ifs' of science and technology. Ian was an integral and indispensable part of The Woman in the Window from the first day.

Alma De Groen
April 1999

In memory of Brian Syron, friend and mentor,
whose advice was always: 'Give it size'.

The Woman in the Window was first produced by Melbourne Theatre Company at The Fairfax, Victorian Arts Centre, Melbourne, on 28 February 1998, with the following cast:

ANNA AKHMATOVA	Julia Blake
LILLI KALINOVSKAYA	Helen Morse
STETSKY	Paul English
RACHEL SEKEROV	Sophie Gregg
AUDITOR	Alex Menglet
KORZH	Alex Menglet
TUSYA	Anne Browning
MIZ	Margaret Mills
MAREN	Margaret Mills
SANDOR VOSS	Paul English

Director, Kate Cherry
Set Designer, Richard Roberts
Costume Designer, Anna French
Composer, Andrew Pendlebury
Lighting Designer, Matt Scott
Dramaturgy, May-Brit Akerholt, Kate Cherry

CHARACTERS

ANNA AKHMATOVA, 62.

RACHEL SEKEROV, early 20s.

LILLI KALINOVSKAYA, 40.

MAREN / MIZ, late 20s / 30s.

TUSYA / 'ELIZA', early 20s.

SANDOR VOSS / STETSKY / 'TARDIGRADE', late 20s.

KORZH / AUDITOR, 40s.

(There is no thematic significance in the doubling, simply an economic consideration.)

All characters except Akhmatova are ficticious. She is regarded by many as having been the greatest woman poet in Western culture. During the decades of the Stalinist Terror she struggled to keep the world alive for the Russian people. She was described as having a regal presence, her gestures, the movement of her hands, her bearing, reflecting an aristocratic past that no longer existed. When she travelled to Tashkent she was recognised for what some believe she truly was: a Holy Woman, a shaman.

SETTING

Leningrad in the early 1950s.

Australia, a future.

ACT ONE

SCENE ONE

Leningrad, 1951. Night and stars. AKHMATOVA *and* LILLI *out walking.*

AKHMATOVA: I'll tell you something Nadya used to do for Osip: their room was even smaller than ours, and Osip needed privacy in order to write. In winter Nadya couldn't sit outside, and he couldn't write with her in the room… so if there was a poem coming on—even if it was ten in the morning—she would yawn and say, 'Oh, I'm so tired, Osip… I think I need a little nap!' And she would lie on the bed with her back to him and pretend to sleep—just to give him the illusion of being alone.

LILLI: I'm perfectly willing to sit out on the stairs, Anna.

AKHMATOVA: It wouldn't help. I waited last night and the Muse didn't come. She comes so seldom now. And if she does, she sits in a corner and stares at me. What's the point of a silent Muse? She wants an effort I can't make any more.

LILLI: Yes, you can. You're doing the most important work there is.

STETSKY *appears in the background.*

AKHMATOVA: Which makes it even harder.

LILLI: Then I won't say it any more.

AKHMATOVA: Say it, Lilli. I need it.

STETSKY *lights a cigarette.*

What other country respects poetry as we do? People are killed for it. Osip. Kolya—

LILLI *looks up.*

LILLI: I find the night sky comforting, don't you…?

AKHMATOVA: Not particularly. No hope of rescue there.

LILLI: It's the only pure thing left. Even our Great Leader can't destroy the sky.

AKHMATOVA: He'd give it a damn good try.

LILLI: He's not omnipotent. He doesn't own the stars.

AKHMATOVA: No, but he owns our sight of them.

LILLI: There's a story going round about an actor. When the Secret Police arrested him they asked his name and he said, 'My name was Boris Barshovsky'. They asked his address and he said, 'I lived on the Fontanka'. They asked his occupation, and he said, 'I was an actor'. He put everything in the past tense—and out of sheer perversity they let him go. It's probably not true, but it's a good story.

AKHMATOVA: It's a Russian story. And they probably arrested him again the next day. [*She shivers.*] Why does it take more and more horror to feel anything, Lilli? One imagines the guards opening the doors of that cattle truck when it reached Siberia and finding their prisoners entombed in a wall of ice, and wonders what they felt? Did they feel anything? I'm not sure I would have—only a sort of bemused wonder. And Meyerhold's wife? They took out her eyes. All I could think was, what did they do with them? Did they leave them in the apartment with the body, or take them away? And if so, what did they do with the eyes? They want us to die while we're still alive.

They exit.

SCENE TWO

Australia. A warning siren sounds in short threatening bursts. A follow spot captures RACHEL. *A voice comes over a public address system.*

VOICE: Stay where you are!

RACHEL *turns, panic stricken, disorientated.*

RACHEL: What have I done? I haven't done anything wrong!

VOICE: Resistance will be a further violation.

RACHEL: My tracer went random! I'm trying to go home!

VOICE: What sector?

RACHEL: 58B!

VOICE: You're in 47C.

RACHEL: It looks like 58B! I went to my room—I thought it was my room—and someone else answered—

VOICE: Name?

RACHEL: Rachel Sekerov.

VOICE: Do you have employment?

RACHEL: Conference stress consultant. Is this a test?

VOICE: A test?

RACHEL: To see how I react?

VOICE: Follow the yellow line to the nearest security centre.

RACHEL: I want to go home!

VOICE: Security will verify if a tracer malfunctioned. Follow the yellow line.

> RACHEL *obeys. She exits. Blackout.*

SCENE THREE

MGB interview room, Leningrad, 1951. KORZH *and* STETSKY *enter with* TUSYA. STETSKY *takes notes.*

KORZH: Tell me about the people next door to you.

TUSYA: Which people?

KORZH: Anna Akhmatova and Lilli Kalinovskaya.

TUSYA: I don't know them. We've just moved in.

KORZH: Who visits them?

TUSYA: I don't know.

KORZH: When? How often? Are they from outside Leningrad?

TUSYA: I don't know!

KORZH: Do they talk in whispers?

TUSYA: Whispers?

KORZH: They're in the room next to you and your husband.

TUSYA: I'm a teacher. I'm busy. I don't see anybody. Or listen.

KORZH: You share a kitchen with them, don't you? And a bathroom?

TUSYA: Yes.

KORZH: Don't they eat? Don't they shit? What are they? Ghosts?

TUSYA: I hardly know them.

KORZH: Lilli Kalinovskaya was a colleague of yours.

TUSYA: In another department.

KORZH: Your husband Yuri's a nuclear physicist… Difficult profession with so many prohibitions… Does he remember all of them, do you think? Why was Lilli Kalinovskaya dismissed?

TUSYA: A student denounced her.

KORZH: For what?

TUSYA: You know the answers.

KORZH: I want to hear your answers.

TUSYA: For using a copy of Comrade Stalin's *Short Course* to prop open a window.

KORZH: Thank you.

TUSYA: You know what a hot summer it's been—

KORZH: Why is Lilli Kalinovskaya living with Anna Akhmatova?

TUSYA: Her landlord threw her out when she lost her job. Akhmatova took her in.

KORZH: What is Lilli Kalinovskaya doing for Akhmatova? Is she helping her in any way?

TUSYA: She's taken over the shopping and the cooking, if that's what you mean. She says Akhmatova doesn't eat unless someone reminds her.

KORZH: What is Lilli Kalinovskaya living on?

TUSYA: I don't know. I expect she's looking for another job.

KORZH: Did you see any papers in the room?

TUSYA: Papers?

KORZH: Note paper. Manuscripts. Poems.

TUSYA: I haven't seen the room.

Blackout. They exit. Bells chime.

SCENE FOUR

Lights come up on AKHMATOVA *at her window.*

SCENE FIVE

Lights up on RACHEL *and* MIZ. MIZ *delivers a free association test, consulting a tiny hand-held computer, or a piece of smart paper, which supplies the questions and evaluates* RACHEL's *answers.* RACHEL *answers confidently without hesitation.*

MIZ: Economics—

RACHEL: Meaning.

MIZ: Nature—
RACHEL: Man.
MIZ: Civilisation—
RACHEL: Rational.
MIZ: History—
RACHEL: Irrelevant.
MIZ: Access—
RACHEL: Forbidden.
MIZ: Moon—
RACHEL: Useful.
MIZ: Earth—
RACHEL: Home.
MIZ: Sex—
RACHEL: Work.
MIZ: Excellent.
RACHEL: Me.

MIZ *corrects her.*

MIZ: Excellent, Rachel.
RACHEL: [*an irrepressible grin*] I know.

MIZ *smiles in spite of herself.*

MIZ: [*unexpectedly*] Technocracy.
RACHEL: Hope.

A silence. She finds MIZ *staring at her.*

MIZ: Hope, Rachel? Why would you need hope? Is there something you're not satisfied with?
RACHEL: [*shocked at herself*] No, Miz.
MIZ: Get focused, Rachel. You're one of the lucky five per cent with a job. I trust you're up to date with your client research?
RACHEL: Yes, Miz.
MIZ: I don't want a repeat of last month when Maren went through an entire two weeks of the Launch Analysts' Conference thinking mass drivers were a religious organisation.
RACHEL: No, Miz.
MIZ: You girls are expected to display empathy as well as good looks and I remind you thousands of girls are striving to take your place.

You have half an hour's downtime—use it wisely.

They exit. AKHMATOVA *leaves the window.*

SCENE SIX

Lights up on a tea table. AKHMATOVA, LILLI *and* TUSYA. TUSYA *nervously examines the room.*

LILLI: How's school, Tusya?

TUSYA: The history books are being rewritten. There's not much to do. The students don't want to study it when it changes so often. They'd rather a subject like yours.

LILLI: [*pretending it would be something wonderful*] What makes you think maths can't change? Our Great Leader could declare pi to be three and raise an entire generation who think circles are hexagons.

> TUSYA *behaves as if she hasn't heard. She examines a drawing of* AKHMATOVA.

TUSYA: [*to* AKHMATOVA] Is this the famous Modigliani portrait? It doesn't look anything like you.

AKHMATOVA: Forty years ago it was thought to have captured me rather well.

TUSYA: A long time.

AKHMATOVA: Another century.

TUSYA: Forty years ago would have been 1911, wouldn't it?

AKHMATOVA: The true twentieth century began in 1914, child, and no one's ever going to convince me otherwise.

TUSYA: He's famous in the West now.

AKHMATOVA: Of course he is. I predicted it.

TUSYA: The glass is cracked.

AKHMATOVA: He showed me Paris in the moonlight. We strolled in the Luxembourg Gardens reciting Verlaine.

TUSYA: [*replacing the picture*] You should have it fixed. If an insect got in—

AKHMATOVA: He was too poor to hire chairs.

> TUSYA *sits.*

TUSYA: You had to pay to sit down?

LILLI *pours tea for her.*

AKHMATOVA: A bench was free.

TUSYA: Disgusting. Treating human beings like that...

AKHMATOVA: That's the way things were.

TUSYA: Were you in love with him?

AKHMATOVA: Supremely.

TUSYA: And I suppose you never saw him again?

AKHMATOVA: On the contrary. One doesn't need a physical presence in order to meet.

LILLI: There's a stream of people through here day and night—Pushkin, Shelley, Dante—

TUSYA: I see. [*She doesn't. To* AKHMATOVA] Yuri and I... we wondered if you and Lilli would have supper with us? Yuri queued for some smoked herring.

AKHMATOVA: Don't you want time to get settled?

TUSYA: There were some stains on the floor but I cleaned those up. And I've put rugs over all the holes. Yuri queued for three hours thinking, 'A famous poet will be eating this'.

AKHMATOVA: Famous this and famous that. What does it mean and what does it matter?

A silence.

TUSYA: Such a beautiful old tea set.

AKHMATOVA: One changes husbands, not china. This should see me through a fourth.

LILLI: Anna!

AKHMATOVA: Why not? It takes courage to visit me. Weeds out the undesirables.

LILLI: Not all of them. [*To* TUSYA] I'm afraid there's no sugar.

TUSYA: That's all right. We haven't any either. Who's reading *The Cherry Orchard*?

LILLI: I am. Anna Andreyevna doesn't appreciate Chekhov.

AKHMATOVA: On the contrary... [*picking up the book*] if it weren't for people like these, we wouldn't be enjoying the sort of life we're enjoying now.

She tosses the book aside.

LILLI: Generous to a fault.

AKHMATOVA: I need the clash of swords when I go to the theatre. Heroism! Spectacle! If I want timidity I can walk down the street.

TUSYA: Yuri and I had a marvellous treat last night: we saw *Anna Karenina*.

AKHMATOVA: Dreadful production. The old nobility never dressed like that—flashy shoes and hats. They were dark and buttoned-up.

TUSYA: I thought it was very effective—it showed how greedy and superficial the aristocracy were.

AKHMATOVA: If one can't be truthful, don't perform the work.

LILLI: What's truthful? Not performing it at all, so no one knows it exists?

AKHMATOVA: The story's a lie in any case.

TUSYA *stares.*

LILLI: What do you mean, a lie?

AKHMATOVA: Anna Karenina herself is a lie. When she lives with Karenin she leads a morally blameless life, even though her husband revolts her; but when she goes to live with Vronsky, who's young and handsome, and whom she loves, she turns into a shameless hussy who'll flirt with anyone. Now ask yourself why Tolstoy makes her do that?

LILLI: She's insecure. She's afraid Vronsky doesn't love her any more. He's bored.

AKHMATOVA: No, it's that rubbishy old man trying to make us believe a woman who leaves her husband automatically turns into a whore. He not only makes her behave like a whore, he has her believing she is, and that Vronsky can't really love her. He does love her.

LILLI: I think he's stopped.

AKHMATOVA: After she kills herself he says: 'My life is loathsome to me. My life has no value.'

LILLI: [*looking at* TUSYA] Some people have argued that was a guilty conscience.

AKHMATOVA: Nonsense. He goes on a suicidal mission to fight the Turks. He throws his life away because he loves her. One kills oneself out of love, not out of a guilty conscience—otherwise we'd have mass suicides up and down the country. The whole book's based on a dishonest psychological premise. It's the morality of Tolstoy's Moscow aunts.

LILLI: [*to* TUSYA] Anna Andreyevna can appreciate Tolstoy almost as much as she appreciates Chekhov.

AKHMATOVA: And look how accurate he was: high-level Petersburg bureaucrats behaving like provincial policemen—

A fine drift of plaster falls from the ceiling. LILLI *looks up. She puts a finger to her lips and gets up. Watching* TUSYA, *she moves aside a bookcase. Concealed behind it is a crude listening device.*

LILLI: [*pointing towards the ceiling*] Riddled with 'vermin'. You might want to check your room as well.

She replaces the bookcase and sits down. TUSYA *looks as if she might faint. She pushes her cup away and gets up.*

TUSYA: I don't think I've had a problem with 'vermin' before.

LILLI: Perhaps you should reconsider your lease?

TUSYA: It took us forever to find this place! Yuri loves the idea of living near other scientists!

LILLI: Fortunately there's a locked door between us and the 'Institute of Popular Science'. If anyone came in the night there'd be time to get dressed.

AKHMATOVA: Providing one had the presence of mind.

TUSYA: No one gives away their room without good reason—

LILLI: Semyon Pavlovitch had a very good reason: they arrested him.

TUSYA *stares in horror.*

TUSYA: People could think we got his room because we knew him!

LILLI: Don't worry, he was harmless. An ordinary criminal.

TUSYA: What did he do?

AKHMATOVA: Strangled his wife. We can contribute some boiled potatoes tonight if that's any help.

LILLI: Are you sure you wouldn't like a little more time to settle in, Tusya?

TUSYA: Yes. A little more time. Perhaps in a week or two.

She goes.

AKHMATOVA: Such a radiant, inquisitive child.

LILLI *picks up her book.*

LILLI: Pity about the herring.

They remain at the table.

SCENE SEVEN

RACHEL *coaches* MAREN.

MAREN: Don't speak too fast.

RACHEL: Slowly.

MAREN: Don't speak too slowly.

RACHEL: Nine?

MAREN: Don't speak too fast.

RACHEL: Easy to get them reversed. Ten?

MAREN: Listen attentively.

RACHEL: Eleven?

MAREN: Don't contradict him.

RACHEL: Twelve?

MAREN: Don't ask highly personal questions. Physical intimacy is not personal intimacy.

RACHEL: Thirteen?

MAREN: Don't volunteer highly personal information about yourself.

RACHEL: Fourteen?

MAREN: Don't criticise.

RACHEL: Fifteen?

MAREN: Listen attentively.

RACHEL: That was ten. Fifteen?

MAREN: Smile—

RACHEL: Smiling is Section Two.

MAREN: Smile when you're introduced! Smile when you speak! Smile when you listen—

RACHEL: Section Two, Maren!

MAREN: —Smile as if your job depended on it. Because it does!

RACHEL: I'm trying to help you.

MAREN: It doesn't matter about the assessment. I could get everything right and still fail the Eigenface!

RACHEL: No, you won't. We'll do some relaxation exercises.

MAREN: You're wasting your downtime for nothing.

RACHEL: When I was new here, you were the one who helped me. No one else worried about me. You'll feel better in the morning. I always do.

> MAREN *exits*. RACHEL *sits, putting on her ractive goggles*. LILLI *lights a candle*. AKHMATOVA *is writing in her notebook*.

SCENE EIGHT

AKHMATOVA *finishes writing*.

AKHMATOVA: [*tearing a page from the notebook*] What a hot summer it's been…

> She hands the page to LILLI. LILLI *reads, memorising*.

> Autumn's come so late this year…
> Such a lon-n-g summer…
> So beautiful…

> LILLI *hands back the page from the notebook*.

[*Whispering*] Are you sure?

> LILLI *nods*.

Let's have some tea…

> AKHMATOVA *strikes a match and sets the poem alight. She drops it in an ashtray. They watch it burn.* LILLI *blows out the candle. She exits.* AKHMATOVA *remains*.

SCENE NINE

RACHEL *is enjoying the ractive, unaware as* MAREN *approaches.* MAREN *prods* RACHEL *to get her attention.* RACHEL *removes the goggles.*

MAREN: [*touching her hair*] Can you see?

RACHEL: What have you done, Maren?

MAREN: I wanted to chop it all off. I wanted to hack and hack at it!

RACHEL: But you stopped.

MAREN: I can't do this any more.

RACHEL: Yes you can. It's hardly visible.

MAREN: I'm finished, Rachel.

RACHEL: Stop shaking, Maren. You know the room reads it. [*Taking her hands*] Hold onto me.

MAREN: Remember the composers…? Mine played me some music—it was like someone trapped in an isolation chamber. The music was how I feel—as if I'm clawing to get out! [*She shows her hands.*] Perfect… but my mind is raw. Scraped. Bleeding.

RACHEL: So we learn things from them… that's what makes being a Conference Girl interesting—

MAREN: It makes their lives interesting, not ours.

RACHEL: Nobody's life's interesting if you think about it.

MAREN: Don't think, Rachel. Wake up every morning with a pillow over your face like I used to. Let time crawl. No thoughts, ideas, feelings…

RACHEL: Find something else!

MAREN: Servicing lower and lower ranks…? I'd rather be nothing. Not a thing. Nothing. I tried to find him again and they're gone. All of them.

RACHEL: Who?

MAREN: The composers. De-listed. They say computers do a better job now.

RACHEL: What is it you want, Maren?

MAREN: A soul. Don't laugh.

RACHEL: I'm not laughing. I don't know what you mean.

MAREN: I want to be allowed my own thoughts!—No Eigenface monitoring every smile—

RACHEL: But it doesn't listen to us—we can still talk to each other!

MAREN: Rachel, when I'm dead I'll be more alive than here.

RACHEL: Everyone has bad days. It could be anything—childhood, or hormones—and bang. Ask Miz for a remedy.

MAREN: I've tried remedies. [*She hesitates.*] Rachel, I'm leaving you my room.

RACHEL: You can't do that—it'll be reassigned.

MAREN: My virtual room. It's mine, I created it. And it helped me at first.

RACHEL: [*bewildered*] Helped how?

MAREN: I want someone to know I existed.

She exits. RACHEL *stares after her, distressed. She follows. The sound of chimes.* AKHMATOVA *crosses to the window.*

SCENE TEN

The street outside AKHMATOVA*'s room.* KORZH *and* STETSKY *enter.*

STETSKY: Call this police work?

KORZH: What's your idea of police work? Eavesdropping on trains?

STETSKY: It was better than this.

KORZH: Let me tell you about Akhmatova, country boy. She's more dangerous than a bomb.

AKHMATOVA: We know what trembles in the balance, what we're called upon to do—

KORZH: They lifted the ban on her during the war and she wrote a poem for the siege of Leningrad—

AKHMATOVA: If we have nothing else, we have courage,
      And courage is required to meet this hour
      Bullets will not deter us
      Courage will not fail

KORZH: Banned for thirty years and every soldier in the trenches knew her words by heart.

AKHMATOVA: We will defend the Russian word
      We will preserve you, great Russian word—
      For our children's songs.

    STETSKY *is staring at* KORZH *with suspicion.*

STETSKY: The war's over.

KORZH: Lose any family in the siege of Leningrad, country boy?

STETSKY: No.

KORZH: I lost my mother and sister. They lived on grass and soup made of carpenters' glue, but they were never starved of words. [*He looks up at* AKHMATOVA.] She knew what to say when we needed courage. She wrote poems that sounded like bells for the whole nation.

    AKHMATOVA *stands, remote, regal, forbidding.*

They call her the Empress of Russia.

STETSKY: So we shoot her and go home.

KORZH: We appear, Anna Akhmatova appears. Twice a day, every day, three hundred and sixty-five days a year.

STETSKY: Why?

KORZH: If she's killed herself or fled the country, she can't stand in a window for us, can she?

STETSKY: Suppose not.

KORZH: And if she doesn't appear—if she's not there at the specified time—Comrade Stalin will want to know immediately. Understand?

STETSKY: Yes, Comrade Lieutenant!

KORZH: When she leaves the building, you follow her. Think you can handle that?

STETSKY: Yes, Comrade Lieutenant.

KORZH: Until there's another order, we just watch.

They exit.

AKHMATOVA: I feel I should chime the hour.

She exits. Lighting change.

SCENE ELEVEN

Lights up on RACHEL *and* MIZ.

MIZ: Define poetry for me, Rachel.

RACHEL: Poetry is words put together so people can remember them easily. There's short lines and sometimes words at the ends of lines rhyme with words at the end of other lines to make it easier to remember what comes next. Also it's old. Poetry is more than a hundred years old.

MIZ: Thousands. Poetry can be thousands of years old. Try to make these men as comfortable as you would the commanders of space stations.

RACHEL: Miz, if they're only low priority, why are they allowed to conference in person?

MIZ: Registered poets have that privilege. It's necessary for their work—or so they claim. They tend to argue when they get together, so watch out for wounded egos. Yours shouldn't have a problem in that regard: he comes from a very important family. That's why I'm entrusting him to you. [*She steps back and studies* RACHEL *approvingly.*] Good. Get through the next two weeks with the grace and efficiency I know you're capable of and no complaints from your client.

RACHEL: I watched you when Maren died. You said to yourself, 'Good girl'.

MIZ: In that one respect, she was a good girl. She did the only thing she could.

RACHEL: Couldn't you have found her something else?

MIZ: She'd stopped doing client research. And she cut a piece of her hair without permission.

RACHEL: Why did she want to die?

MIZ: Why didn't she want to live? No one gets left behind in this world unless they choose to be left, not if they're lucky enough to have work. Maren chose to be unhappy. Your Eigenface analysis—

RACHEL: [*tensing*] Yes?

MIZ: Continues to show a genuine smile.

    RACHEL *smiles, relieved.*

RACHEL: Thank you.

MIZ: Thank the computer. It knows. Clients only sense it. You're still our most popular girl. Don't get yourself logged.

    They exit. Lighting change.

SCENE TWELVE

AKHMATOVA *and* LILLI *rush in.* LILLI *puts a teapot on the table.*

LILLI: You're sure they're coming in?

    AKHMATOVA *is gathering pages of typescript and stuffing them behind books on a shelf.*

AKHMATOVA: I'm sure. Answer everything. If all they're doing is putting in a report it makes it easier for everyone. Otherwise they'll come back. Perhaps it's just attrition. We were too safe.

Deliberately, she teases a scrap of typescript out until it protrudes a little between two books, clearly visible to anyone who looks closely.

LILLI: Anna, you're mad!

AKHMATOVA: As the Cheshire Cat said to Alice: 'I'm mad, you're mad, we're all mad here'! Sanity depends on it.

She sits in her chair.

LILLI: Have you got Dante?

AKHMATOVA: My entire conscious life? Of course I've got him!

LILLI: The portrait! You haven't got the portrait!

AKHMATOVA: It's too late.

LILLI: [*getting it*] It's not too late.

She unfastens AKHMATOVA*'s suitcase, puts the portrait in and fastens the case again. She joins* AKHMATOVA *at the table.*

My bowels are exploding.

AKHMATOVA: Hold it in.

KORZH *and* STETSKY *enter. A silence as* KORZH *stands taking in the spartan room. He turns and looks at the women.*

KORZH: Good afternoon. Your papers, please.

The women hand over their papers. STETSKY *runs his hands expertly over* LILLI, *checking her pockets. He turns towards* AKHMATOVA. *She draws herself up imperiously.*

AKHMATOVA: I've had enough excitement in my life, young man. I don't need you to liven it up.

He stops, intimidated.

KORZH: Check their shoes, country boy.

LILLI *removes her shoes.* STETSKY *examines the lining.* KORZH *looks at their papers.*

What kind of a name is Akhmatova?

AKHMATOVA: A Tartar name.

KORZH: Your own?

AKHMATOVA: I was born Gorenko.

KORZH: Why the change?

AKHMATOVA: My father was embarrassed by a daughter writing poetry. I took the name of my great grandmother.

KORZH: Who was…?

AKHMATOVA: A Tartar princess. A descendant of the Golden Horde.

STETSKY: You're descended from Genghis Khan? Why doesn't that surprise me?

He gives LILLI *her shoes and turns reluctantly to* AKHMATOVA. *She hands him hers. Under her steady gaze, he looks at them self-consciously and hands them back.*

KORZH: What are you living on?

AKHMATOVA: After I was expelled from the Writer's Union people began sending me food coupons. I eat, courtesy of 'Anonymous'.

STETSKY *is pulling books from the shelf, shaking them out, peering down the spines, then tossing them on the floor.*

KORZH: I assume you have the six-volume edition of Lenin and the collected edition of Stalin?

LILLI: Certainly.

STETSKY *has inadvertently thrown them on the floor.* LILLI *pointedly retrieves one and hands it to him. He hurriedly collects the others and returns them to the shelf, giving* KORZH *a frightened look.* KORZH *picks up a book.*

KORZH: *Flatland?*

LILLI: It's a Euclidean universe inhabited by two-dimensional caricatures of English society. Mathematicians use it to illustrate the difficulty of dealing with ideas that transcend our understanding.

KORZH: What ideas?

LILLI: Events in a higher dimension.

KORZH: English society?

LILLI: No, no, they're in a lower dimension.

KORZH *tosses the book aside.* LILLI *picks it up.* KORZH *looks about the room.*

KORZH: This is sad to see, Anna Andreyevna. Very sad. [*With sincere regret*] You could do so much for your country. We could do so much for you: a dacha in the writers' colony, travel abroad… wherever your country needs you to go. You could have a house like Gorki's.

AKHMATOVA: I should be like Gorki?

KORZH: He is honoured.

AKHMATOVA: I do not need his kind of honour.

STETSKY *finds the typed pages.*

STETSKY: What are these? [*Handing the pages to* KORZH] It looks like typing—

AKHMATOVA: I like to think so. My publisher may not.

KORZH: This is poetry!

AKHMATOVA: I have reservations about that, but some might agree with you.

KORZH: Yours?

AKHMATOVA: Of course not mine. It's a translation from Victor Hugo.

KORZH: You have permission for this?

AKHMATOVA: I have a contract.

KORZH: But the pages were hidden.

AKHMATOVA: Not hidden. I simply don't care to be reminded of them.

KORZH: You dislike this work?

AKHMATOVA: Translation? It's like eating one's own brain.

LILLI: The writers without talent are free to write; the writers with talent are free to translate.

KORZH *puts the pages in his pocket.*

KORZH: If your poetry isn't being published any more, it's because it isn't useful. Comrade Stalin tells us life must be depicted as it should be, not as it is. [*He feels the teapot. It's hot. He pours himself some tea.*] Yes… we live in the present, but we look at it from our glorious future. During the war your poems were valuable, but most of your work… was too personal. There's no personal life any more. You wrote about nature too—

AKHMATOVA: There's no nature any more?

KORZH: [*continuing*] It's no way to turn us into a great economic power. Poetry needs to pay its way like everything else. [*He removes one of* AKHMATOVA's *china plates and pockets it. He turns to* STETSKY.] Bring them.

Shocked, the women reach out to each other instinctively and clasp hands. STETSKY *looks uncertainly from* AKHMATOVA *and* LILLI *to* KORZH.

The *books*!

STETSKY gathers the books from the floor.

Comrade Stalin believes writers are engineers of human souls. We need our greatest writers to describe what we are doing.

He exits. STETSKY *finishes picking up the books. He clicks his fingers at* LILLI *who is still holding* Flatland. *She hands it over.* STETSKY *exits.* AKHMATOVA *picks up* The Cherry Orchard *and starts after them.*

AKHMATOVA: Wait! You forgot Chekhov!

Lighting change. AKHMATOVA *and* LILLI *exit as:*

SCENE THIRTEEN

Behind a scrim, two women burn a poem. As the flame dies down, RACHEL *and* SANDOR *enter in darkness.* RACHEL, *facing upstage, replaces her dress as the lights come up.* SANDOR *reclines on pillows, shoes off, chest bare, watching her.* MIZ *enters with a jug of wine and two glasses. She casts an appraising glance at* RACHEL.

MIZ: [*to* SANDOR] I trust everything meets with your approval?
SANDOR: Absolutely.

RACHEL gives him a dazzling smile. MIZ *puts the wine down.*

MIZ: Rachel is without question our most popular girl. If you have any problems—
SANDOR: No, no. Everything's fine.
MIZ: All of our girls are highly trained professionals, Mr Voss, perfect in every way. If there is anything not to your liking, please let me know.

She exits. A silence. RACHEL *pours the wine and hands a glass to* SANDOR. *She sits next to him.*

RACHEL: Is this your first visit to Earth?
SANDOR: No, I've been coming here since I was a child. My parents thought it would help me appreciate how lucky I am.
RACHEL: I've never been on a space station.
SANDOR: Never?

RACHEL: I've only ever travelled virtually. But I'm going to one day. I'm determined.

SANDOR: My family makes wine… [*He lifts the glass to his nose. Grimacing*] Not a bouquet I've encountered before…

RACHEL: It's made from plankton.

He hands her the glass without tasting it.

SANDOR: We make ours from real grapes. My people originally came from the Barossa Valley. We supply the entire top rank.

RACHEL: Miz says you come from a very important family.

SANDOR: [*surveying the room*] You've no idea… At home on the space station there's green… vineyards to walk through. Along the axis there's zero gravity—as a child I used to strap on wings and fly.

RACHEL: Tell me more about up there.

SANDOR: On a space station? You must have heard about it from hundreds of people.

RACHEL: Not from a poet.

SANDOR: I'm on the outer belt, so we see Earth through a kind of haze— but the stars are all visible.

RACHEL: I've never seen them.

SANDOR: No. Suppose you wouldn't have.

RACHEL: How do you find your way home through millions of space stations?

SANDOR: Same way you find your room, except it's a homing device on a shuttle.

RACHEL: One day my tracer went random. Took me to the wrong sector. I beeped my room—a girl came out who looked like me. Everyone knew where they were except me. I thought, what if all the tracers went random?

SANDOR: I've never ended up on the wrong space station.

RACHEL: But you could.

SANDOR: Yes, but it's not likely.

Another silence. RACHEL *gets up.*

RACHEL: Want to see my pet?

He looks surprised. She opens a little box and takes out a tiny cube.

It's only small. A biologist gave him to me.

She hands him the cube. He peers at it.

SANDOR: It certainly is small. I can't even see it in there.

RACHEL: It's a tardigrade. He's very sweet at a hundred times magnification. He's like a little bear with eight legs. He can sleep for a hundred years in suspended animation and live at temperatures hundreds of degrees below freezing. Or you could boil him if you wanted.

SANDOR: Unsurpassed.

RACHEL: The biologist said, 'I think you should have this. It's an animal that can switch life on and off.'

He hands it back. She returns it to its box and sits beside him again.

We had composers once. You're my first poet.

SANDOR: I specialise in the moon.

RACHEL: Yes, I was going to ask you about that…

He recites:

SANDOR: Cities drowned in olden time
Keep, they say, a magic chime
Rolling up from far below
When the moon-led waters flow.

So within me, ocean deep,
Lies a sunken world asleep.
Lest its bells forget to ring
Memory! Set the tide a-swing![1]

RACHEL: [*applauding*] Oh, that was wonderful! Just lovely!

SANDOR: Understand it?

RACHEL: Some of it. Not all.

SANDOR: What didn't you understand?

RACHEL: The first word?

SANDOR: There used to be areas not populated.

RACHEL: They were cities?

SANDOR: Cities were the bits between that were populated.

---

1   Henry Newbolt (1862–1938), 'Cities Drowned'.

RACHEL: Must have been hardly anyone around. [*Dreamily*] A world within me…

SANDOR: 'So within me, ocean deep,
          Lies a sunken world asleep.'

RACHEL: I expected poetry to be easy… short sentences.

SANDOR: 'Hey diddle diddle,
          The cat and the fiddle,
          The cow jumped over the moon!'

RACHEL: What's a cat…? What's a fiddle? What's a cow—?

SANDOR: I thought you girls were educated.

RACHEL: I'm sorry!—You won't report me for not knowing, will you, Sandor?

SANDOR: Of course not.

RACHEL: Truly?

SANDOR: Don't worry about it.

She smiles, relieved.

RACHEL: Thank you. I could lose my job if you did.

He strokes her body.

I was going to ask why you specialised in the moon? Isn't that an odd subject for a poet?

SANDOR: It looked bigger once; they pushed it further away launching space stations into low earth orbit. At night it was the brightest light in the sky.

RACHEL: Must have been so dark in those days.

SANDOR: There's an old Norse legend: one day the moon will be eaten by a wolf and disappear, and that'll be the end of the world.

RACHEL: How do you know things?

SANDOR: One of the privileges of being a poet: I'm allowed to access the history archives—what's left since the clean-out.

He sees she doesn't comprehend.

Before you were born, countries tried to rebel. It's why a lot of history got cleaned out—deleting and reassigning people's tribal loyalties. We weren't always like this; the corporations only took over when countries couldn't pay their debts.

RACHEL: You must be so clever.

SANDOR: My parents wanted me to create games so I'd always have a job—I didn't have enough imagination. I became a poet instead.

He leans back against the pillows:

'To behold the wandering moon
Riding near her highest noon
Like one that had been led astray
Through the heavens' wide pathless way.'[2]

Did you know that once upon a time poets wrote their own words?

RACHEL: No.

SANDOR: Who do you think created the poems in the first place?

RACHEL: I don't know. I never thought about it.

Blackout. They exit.

SCENE FOURTEEN

Lights up on AKHMATOVA *and* LILLI, *strolling arm in arm.*

LILLI: [*to herself, memorising*] 'For a long time I stood at the gate of Hell
      But Hell was dark—'
[*Uncertainly*] 'But hell was shut—'

AKHMATOVA: Closed.

LILLI: 'For a long time I stood at the gate of Hell
      But Hell was closed
      Even the Devil didn't need me.
      So where should I go?'

SCENE FIFTEEN

SANDOR *enters. He addresses his peers.*

SANDOR: My fellow poets… We have these instincts; a prickle in the back of the neck about someone if we have a true poet's calling. There had to be more. He had it in him to be great. So I got permission to do a deep search—and I found him. He didn't just write love poems, charming though they were. He was there, in the archives, untouched since theatre disappeared. We all know the expression: 'To be, or not to be': friends, I think I can tell you where it came

---

2   John Milton (1608–1674), 'Il Penseroso'.

from. Now, thanks to careful lobbying of the authorities, the plays of William Shakespeare are accessible again, reclassified under poetry. Gentlemen, one thing before I go any further: all references to the moon in his work are off limits. That's my market niche. I leave the rest of the field to you. There's plenty there for everyone.

He exits. The lights go down and stars come up.

SCENE SIXTEEN

AKHMATOVA *and* LILLI *continue their walk.*

AKHMATOVA: Which is worse: believing there's a God who exists alongside this, or believing there's no God, only evil?

LILLI: What do you fear most, Anna?

AKHMATOVA: That I mightn't be able to go on describing this.

LILLI: But you are.

AKHMATOVA: They're saying this is a final purge; after this it won't be necessary for any more. We disappear in categories now—historians one week, mystics the next. People in the West must think I've been struck dumb by it all. As good as, if no one can read me.

LILLI: 'For a long time I stood at the gate of Hell
    But Hell was closed…'

AKHMATOVA: Who needs Gutenberg? We're back in the days of Homer.

LILLI: 'Even the Devil didn't need me.
    So where should I go?'

AKHMATOVA: One more for Natalya to memorise.

LILLI: Natalya's dead.

AKHMATOVA *stops.*

AKHMATOVA: Dead? I put her in the group because she seemed safe! The least likely to be arrested!

LILLI: Pneumonia. I thought you knew.

AKHMATOVA: Pneumonia? I didn't think people were allowed to die of natural causes any more. [*Belatedly*] Poor Natalya.

LILLI: She'll need to be replaced.

AKHMATOVA: Who's left?

LILLI: I'm still here. We were memorising the same poems.

AKHMATOVA: It's too much responsibility for one person.

LILLI: You mean if anything happened to me?

AKHMATOVA: Nothing's going to happen to you, Lilli! You have to remember. I have to find the words. If they knew what I see now, they'd burn me at the stake.

LILLI: What do you see?

AKHMATOVA: A world in a waking dream… I seem to be witnessing a dying world. I'm asked to keep faith with that world and guard it… [*She shivers.*] But who is to guard me?

> *They exit.*

SCENE SEVENTEEN

Outdoors. A Preservation. SANDOR *leads* RACHEL *by the hand. She is hesitant.*

SANDOR: The Earth curves the wrong way—away not up. [*Pointing*] Look—there's nothing. On a space station you look up: you see the other side of the station.

> RACHEL *has her head down.*

The horizon! Look.

> *She covers her eyes.*

You wanted to see a Preservation.

> *She shakes her head.*

RACHEL: My eyes…

SANDOR: Sorry. I didn't think.

RACHEL: Not used to seeing so far.

> *He sits.* RACHEL *hesitates.*

SANDOR: It's grass. It's safe to sit on.

> *He pulls her down after him.*

This was the Snowy Mountains High Country. Currangormbla Plain.

RACHEL: I feel giddy.

SANDOR: Put your head down.

RACHEL: My feet are numb. My legs. Arms. Can't breathe!

SANDOR: Panic attack. Stay calm.

RACHEL: My heart's pounding!

SANDOR: There should be birdsong… something relaxing. I'll turn on the birds.

He touches his tracer: the harsh and deafening sound of kookaburras and cockatoos. RACHEL *cringes, covering her ears.*

Sulphur-crested cockatoos, and kookaburras! Don't know which is which!

RACHEL: Stop it! Please!

Silence.

SANDOR: Sorry.

RACHEL: Not your fault.

SANDOR: [*taking her hand*] Better?

She nods.

RACHEL: Is the grass real?

SANDOR: Yes.

RACHEL: The trees?

SANDOR: I think so.

RACHEL: I could look up.

SANDOR: Not all at once.

She follows the line of the trees and slowly raises her gaze.

RACHEL: It's…

She can't find words.

SANDOR: Blue?

RACHEL: Is that its real colour?

SANDOR: That's the weather. It's whatever colour the weather dictates.

RACHEL: It's so…

SANDOR: Big?

RACHEL: It's ractive!

She puts an arm out, holding onto him as she looks down. She sits slowly, touching the grass experimentally with her hands.

How long can we stay?

SANDOR: An hour.

She lies back and looks up at the sky.

RACHEL: What else?

SANDOR: What would you like?

RACHEL: What did people do in places like this?

He pulls her up and after him. She is awkward, can't adjust to big steps and speed.

What's this?

SANDOR: Running!

They run round and round in circles.

RACHEL: What else?

SANDOR: [*shouting*] Shout!

RACHEL: What?

SANDOR: Your name!

RACHEL: Rachel!

SANDOR: Louder!

RACHEL: Rachel!

SANDOR: [*shouting*] Louder!

RACHEL: RACHEL…! What else?

SANDOR: Anything!

RACHEL: What's the name here?

SANDOR: Currangormbla.

RACHEL: [*shouting*] Currangormbla!

They jump around, shouting the name over and over. The bird sounds start up again. A madness takes hold. RACHEL is laughing. She stops, exhausted, emotional. Bird sounds fade.

SANDOR: What's wrong? Are you giddy again?

She shakes her head. She walks away from him, hiding her face.

What?

He follows her, turns her around.

Why are you crying?

RACHEL: I don't know.

SANDOR: Tell me!

She shakes her head.

Try.

RACHEL: I'm not alive. There's something here that isn't in me. Ask for another girl. I'm sick.

SANDOR: I don't want another girl.

RACHEL: Two weeks, Sandor! You're entitled!

SANDOR: I don't want another girl, Rachel. I want you.

> *Lights fade. Birds screeching in the blackness becomes pounding on an outer door.*

SCENE EIGHTEEN

TUSYA is screaming, 'Yuri!'. A door slams, then there is silence. Lights up on AKHMATOVA and LILLI, clothes thrown on in haste. TUSYA in a nightdress.

TUSYA: What'll I do? What's going to happen to him?

LILLI: Get your bag, Tusya. I'll come to the train with you.

TUSYA: My bag?

LILLI: Didn't you have a suitcase ready?

TUSYA: Of course.

LILLI: Get dressed and we'll go.

TUSYA: What if they let him come home? I can't leave!

LILLI: You have to. They always come back for the wives. But if you disappear for a while they don't look too hard.

TUSYA: Why would they arrest Yuri?

AKHMATOVA: They never say why.

TUSYA: Because he looked at someone the wrong way? Or someone didn't like the way he looked? Or he hummed a tune that shouldn't be hummed? Talked too much, talked too little—said something? So many stupid things have been happening he was bound to say something!

LILLI: What things?

TUSYA: People are getting sick at Chelyabinsk so they've stopped dumping nuclear waste in the river, and now they're diverting it into a lake. The lake is self-contained. Yuri asked what would happen if there's a hot summer and the lake dries up. There'd be radioactive dust blowing for hundreds of miles!

LILLI: Tusya, you have to leave.

TUSYA: [*yelling*] Don't tell me what to do!

LILLI: I thought that was what you wanted.

AKHMATOVA: Leave her alone, Lilli.

> TUSYA *looks down at her nightdress.*

TUSYA: We panicked. They took him in his pyjamas. We should never have moved in here. What neighbours! [*She turns on them.*] Fired for counter-revolutionary activity, and a forbidden poet! [*Shouting at* AKHMATOVA] Everyone around you suffers! Your son's in a labour camp because of you! Why are you still here? You could have emigrated years ago! You had your chance!

AKHMATOVA: Leave my people?

TUSYA: Who says we're your people? We didn't have any say in it!

AKHMATOVA: I believe the people did.

TUSYA: You arrogant old witch!

AKHMATOVA: Who can refuse their own life?

TUSYA: I wish you had! They took him because of you!

> TUSYA *runs out.* LILLI *helps* AKHMATOVA *to a chair.*

AKHMATOVA: It's true. Lev has spent eight years of his life in prison because of me. Go to the train and don't come back.

LILLI: They turn the electricity off hoping you'll fall down the stairs—

AKHMATOVA: I'm warning you, go—and don't tell me where. No more hostages.

LILLI: You could lie there for hours—supposing the fall didn't kill you. You could have another heart attack! I'm not leaving.

> *Blackout. They exit.*

SCENE NINETEEN

Lights start to come up on RACHEL *sitting in a small pool of light, goggled into a ractive.*

RACHEL: Why are you accusing me? It's nothing.

MIZ: [*voice-over*] I'll ask you again, Rachel: what's that in your hand?

RACHEL: Only my pet bear, Miz.

MIZ: [*voice-over*] People like us don't have pets! They eat and they defecate.

RACHEL: My tardigrade's too small to eat or shit, Miz.

MIZ: [*voice-over*] Small! He's HUGE!

RACHEL: He's getting bigger because you've upset him!

TARDIGRADE: [*voice-over, deep growl*] I'm going to eat you and shit you out!

MIZ: [*voice-over, screaming*] No, no! Stop him!

> MIZ *screams and screams.* RACHEL *hugs herself, horrified, enraptured. The stage floods with light. The sound stops.* RACHEL *removes her goggles. The* AUDITOR *enters.*

AUDITOR: Childish. May I offer some advice?

RACHEL: You turned me off!

AUDITOR: Next time it gives you something negative about authority, get out of the story.

RACHEL: As soon as it gets to be fun!

AUDITOR: You can have fun with a fantasy character.

RACHEL: None of it's real, Auditor. It's a ractive!

AUDITOR: Exactly, it's a program: it knows what interests you—it learns. It tries variations until it gets a response from you.

RACHEL: Every ractive?

AUDITOR: Why else is ninety-five per cent of the population goggled in?

RACHEL: What would they do if they weren't?

AUDITOR: The stuff of nightmares. They monitor you—then alert us when you have an inappropriate response. A gleeful reaction to a superior being eaten qualifies as inappropriate.

RACHEL: I didn't know it was trying to trap me like that.

AUDITOR: Unlike the rest of us, you girls aren't chosen for your brains.

RACHEL: I'm stupid?

AUDITOR: [*coming close*] If I had my pick of any of you, it'd be you.

> *He strokes her hair. She flinches.*

I don't have my pick. A poet has a higher ranking than I do. [*Removing the goggles from her hand*] The punishment for this offence is sixteen hours in an isolation chamber.

RACHEL: Can it be overlooked?

AUDITOR: It could carry a lesser charge, Rachel…

> *He puts his hand on her leg and begins to lift her dress.* RACHEL *submits without resistance. Blackout.*

SCENE TWENTY

Night. AKHMATOVA *and* LILLI *in heavy coats outdoors.* STETSKY *loiters, cold and bored.*

LILLI: [*shivering*] We won't be able to do this much longer.

AKHMATOVA: The silence of winter. I'm tired of living in a whisper. This Flatland isn't life. I want to shout to the heavens. I want to shout that there are heavens! Mayakovsky saw a creature no one else saw: a monster, crossing the mountains of time. Everyone thought he meant the twentieth century. Perhaps he saw the future. Am I going mad, Lilli?

LILLI: No, you've been mad for as long as I've known you.

AKHMATOVA: These creatures I see… these phantoms… they're not real, are they?

LILLI: Einstein spoke of curved space-time… perhaps two parts overlap.

AKHMATOVA: Then they exist?

LILLI: It's one possible future, Anna—not necessarily ours. Quantum theory allows for an infinite number.

AKHMATOVA: They seem small. Terrifying creatures, privileged and impoverished at the same time. Two-dimensional shadow people— even though they seem to live in a world without true darkness—

LILLI: Are you speaking of humanity or geometry?

AKHMATOVA: Humanity—I think. [*She shivers.*] But they have no thoughts as we know them. Their thoughts are terrifying.

LILLI: What thoughts?

AKHMATOVA: It's like a dream that can't be recalled… their minds are searching for something they've lost. I don't know if I'm part of their world, or they're in mine.

She is frail, trembling. LILLI *assists her, worried.*

LILLI: Can't you stop?

AKHMATOVA: That would be ungracious, Lilli. They're my guests—just as if they were Shelley or Dante. I have to find out what they want from me.

They exit. Blackout.

SCENE TWENTY-ONE

Lights up on RACHEL *in an isolation chamber. She presses her palms against an unseen barrier in panic. Her voice is muffled, strange.*

RACHEL: There's nothing! Nightmares are better! Nightmares have people! Scratch on the door! Anything! There must be a door! How long? An hour? Five minutes? A day…? Nothing to see…! Nothing to do…! Nothing to think! [*She beats futilely against an unseen wall.*] Say something to me! SAY SOMETHING!

    Blackout.

SCENE TWENTY-TWO

AKHMATOVA *and* LILLI *enter in darkness.*

LILLI: Where did you put the matches, Anna?
AKHMATOVA: Why do you assume I put them somewhere?
LILLI: You were the one smoking.
AKHMATOVA: Look beside the chair.
LILLI: You mean feel.
AKHMATOVA: Even in pitch darkness you have to be precise.

    LILLI *strikes a match.*

LILLI: Now all we need is a candle.

    A torch beam cuts through the darkness. KORZH *walks forward.* STETSKY *follows.*

KORZH: Get your things.
AKHMATOVA: I doubt if I can find them in the dark.
KORZH: Lilli Kalinovskaya.
AKHMATOVA: Lilli?
KORZH: You have two minutes.
AKHMATOVA: There's a mistake!
LILLI: Don't waste time, Anna. [*To* KORZH] My suitcase is near the door. If you'll direct your torch a little to your left…

    KORZH *shines the torch on the case.*

AKHMATOVA: You need food, Lilli! You have to take some food!

LILLI *collects her case.*

LILLI: Never mind now.

AKHMATOVA: She has the wrong shoes! She can't go in those. We've been to the theatre! Let me find her boots!

The men propel LILLI *towards the door.* AKHMATOVA *follows.*

Why are you taking her? This is all wrong! [*She pulls off her fur coat.*] Take this, Lilli! Take it!

LILLI *takes the coat. She drops it on the floor with the suitcase and throws her arms around* AKHMATOVA. *The men separate them.* LILLI *picks up the case and coat and goes out with the two men. The room is dark.* AKHMATOVA *lights a cigarette. The match flares in the darkness and goes out.*

Well, Lilli… Who is going to show me where to put the commas now?

END OF ACT ONE

ACT TWO

SCENE ONE

MGB Headquarters. STETSKY *records in a notebook.*

KORZH: In all the time you've been with Akhmatova you've never seen her write a line?

LILLI: Of course I saw her writing—so did you… Victor Hugo, which I understand Comrade Stalin read as a boy—shopping lists—potatoes feature rather heavily, tins of corn, which for some reason are usually available—

KORZH: I'm speaking of poetry.

LILLI: To the best of my knowledge, Akhmatova hasn't written a line of poetry since her son Lev was arrested, except for the cycle of poems she wrote last year in praise of Stalin, which probably saved her son's life.

> KORZH *pours himself a glass of water and drinks.*

KORZH: In all the time you've been with her you've never seen her writing a line?

LILLI: We've been over and over this.

KORZH: I'm giving you a chance as a citizen to participate in state security.

LILLI: I appreciate the opportunity. How may I help you?

KORZH: Tell me about Akhmatova.

LILLI: She believes life is a gift to be lived no matter how cruel and horrifying. I'm not sure I do any more. She's a woman who knows her own power. There are such people in the world. You can't regulate genius. You can only destroy it.

KORZH: Your landlord overheard her criticising a public official—she said his urine was normal—was that intended as an insult?

LILLI: It sounds more like a medical diagnosis to me.

KORZH: Which Akhmatova is not qualified to make. What do you think she meant by it?

LILLI: I've no idea. Other people's urine is not a subject that interests me on the whole.

KORZH: Who visits her?

LILLI: You know everyone who visits us. [*She looks at* STETSKY.] Are you checking up on your own spies?

KORZH: She seems to have more women about her than men.

LILLI: Funny that. You shot her first husband, sent another to a labour camp, killed her artistic soul-mate, Osip Mandelstam. And then of course there's her son.

KORZH: I see you haven't been able to find work since you lost your job.

LILLI: People haven't been falling over themselves to associate with me, no.

KORZH: What is your position with Akhmatova?

LILLI: Position?

KORZH: What is your function in the household?

LILLI: Shopping, cooking, cleaning—a shoulder to cry on. Anna Andreyevna likes to dress well. I'm good with my hands: I unpicked some dresses that were worn out and made new ones. I mended her underwear, which was in shreds, and her dressing gown. Anything else you'd like to know?

KORZH: Why did she tell Tusya Laskina she'd had contact with the painter Modigliani who is from the West?

LILLI: Poor Tusya.

KORZH: You feel sorry for that informer?

LILLI: I feel sorry for all of us. I feel sorry for you.

KORZH: Answer the question. Was there a visitor we don't know about?

LILLI: Can you legislate against people's dreams? Akhmatova has many such visitors.

KORZH: From the West?

LILLI: From the dead.

KORZH: Are you saying she's some sort of shaman? Or psychic?

LILLI: I'm saying she's a lonely woman who's saved what remains of her sanity by not setting limits to her mind and soul. Exploring other dimensions isn't confined to mystics—they're rather thin on the ground now in any case—no, she's right up there with quantum physicists on that score. The Russian people have been 'protected' from Akhmatova for almost thirty years, 'protected' from one of the few people left who can make our history coherent for us: a crime committed by the State against its own people, along with so many other crimes.

KORZH: [*to* STETSKY] Are you getting this down?

STETSKY: Yep. Trying…

KORZH: Something happened to your vocabulary, country boy?

STETSKY: I'm sorry, Comrade Lieutenant.

KORZH: [*to* LILLI] Your word count doesn't appear in need of enhancement.

LILLI: I've heard people called in for a 'chat' sometimes feel relief at having a chance to speak freely.

KORZH: You consider you're speaking freely?

LILLI: I'm a little rusty, but give me time. I was ten when all this began. I spake as a child. Today I'm planning a positive orgy of free speech for probably the first and last time in my life. I could, for instance, recite a list of the known dead—a list of those I loved who were taken from me. My husband was sentenced to ten years without right of correspondence. I've since learned what that means. A dear colleague died because he had the same surname as Trotsky. Children of twelve can be arrested. They don't even know why. The parents don't know why. Perhaps I could list the accomplishments of our Great Leader: remembering the name, address, telephone number and family tree of anyone who ever annoyed him or got in his way… taking the exponential increase out of population growth and perfecting a kind of reverse eugenics where the brave and the good are weeded out.

> STETSKY *continues to write frantically.*

You say 'a little violence now' will obviate the need for further violence later on. You believe in a perfectly engineered, scientifically determined future, but science doesn't believe in you. For suggesting there might be problems with the unrestricted release of radio-active waste you've put scientists in prison. We were safer under Hitler's bombs than we are now. Nothing means anything any more because we no longer believe in a future. Do you think this can go on without consequences?

> KORZH *takes the glass from the table. Facing upstage he unbuttons himself and urinates in the glass, comes back and hands the glass to* LILLI.

Interesting. Shamans in Siberia do this, did you know? Of course

the donor is expected to have ingested large amounts of psycho-
active mushrooms. I believe the 'flow-on' effect can be enjoyed by
up to six people. I don't know that this will do much for me. What
did you have for breakfast?

She drinks. Immediately, her body betrays her. She vomits.

KORZH: You're not going to cut this short by provoking me.

He pushes her down and rubs her face in the vomit.

It appears you have no close surviving relatives.

LILLI: [*gasping*] Part of Comrade Stalin's program to lower the national
I.Q.!

He pulls her up by the hair and looks at STETSKY.

KORZH: Always assume that existing procedures are too lax.

Blackout. They exit.

SCENE TWO

Lights up on AKHMATOVA.

AKHMATOVA: We danced and made love on the edge of an inferno. We
tumbled into Terror in our Carnival masks and our satin shoes.
There were people starving, who had no shelter, who couldn't read,
and we didn't care. Are we part of humanity—or just some awful
lesson? No one knows the era they're living in until it's too late.

Lights fade.

Alex Menglet as Korzh and Helen Morse as Lilli Kalinovskaya in the 1998 Melbourne Theatre Company production. (Photo: Jeff Busby)

SCENE THREE

RACHEL *and* SANDOR *enter* MAREN*'s virtual room.*

RACHEL: Maren left me this before she died. I don't understand. What's so special? Why have a virtual room that's dark? What's the use?

SANDOR: So many questions.

RACHEL: There's nothing here.

SANDOR: Look.

> *Stars are beginning to appear: the night sky in the Southern Hemisphere.*

RACHEL: Stars? But they're not real!

SANDOR: Your body doesn't know that. When you look up, your eyes don't know that. Your body responds to what the senses feed it as real. Look, you can see the Southern Cross.

> 'Look at all the fire-folk, sitting in the air!'[3]

RACHEL: They're not people.

SANDOR: The stars were beacons. Maps. People found their way home by them. Great voyages across oceans…

RACHEL: Maren said this helped.

SANDOR: Because she was alone here. I think we're not meant to talk. I think I'm not meant to be here at all.

RACHEL: You're going? Don't go!

SANDOR: She meant you to be by yourself. She left you a gift, Rachel: the night sky as it used to be. Accurate, as far as I can tell. Someone must have given her access to the science archives.

RACHEL: Let's leave.

SANDOR: You're frightened?

RACHEL: [*lying*] No.

SANDOR: I'll stay with you.

RACHEL: That poem—a world within me that's asleep: Maren found that world. Look what happened. I feel things! How do I make sense of things?—who I am… whether this is all there is?—or is there some other kind of life…? whether if I banged my head against the side of my crib long enough I might think different thoughts!

SANDOR: What thoughts?

---

3   Gerard Manley Hopkins (1844–1889), 'The Starlight Night'.

RACHEL: Different thoughts! If I knew I'd already be thinking them!

> *They are slowly bathed in a radiance.* RACHEL *stares, stunned and awed as the moon begins to rise.* SANDOR *leaves.*

SCENE FOUR

RACHEL *remains in the virtual room. Faintly, the sound of church bells.* AKHMATOVA*'s unlit room is flooded with moonlight/starlight from the virtuality.*

RACHEL: [*remembering*] Shouting was wonderful... better than the sky. I want to shout that there are heavens!

> AKHMATOVA *searches and finds a bottle and pours herself a drink. She toasts the moon.*

AKHMATOVA: To a New Year and new sorrow. [*She drinks.*] The most reliable thing on earth—sorrow.

> LILLI *appears.*

[*Softly*] Is the new moon making fun of me...? It's not you, is it?—between the cupboard and the stair...? Pale forehead, staring eyes... Can gravestones melt...? Is granite softer than wax...? Well, Lilli, there's no one left to lose now. Should I be glad of that? Perhaps now it might be possible to weep.

LILLI: Don't drink so much.

AKHMATOVA: Vodka's good for a bad heart. Enlarges the arteries. [*She toasts.*] I drink to our ruined country... to our cruel lives... to the loneliness we shared...

LILLI: Have you found my replacement yet?

AKHMATOVA: Lilli, I've barely found where you hid the tea. Pushkin knew what he was doing—how to stop when he'd said all there was to say.

LILLI: Have you said everything?

AKHMATOVA: Can words be adequate after this?

LILLI: Yours tend to be more than adequate.

AKHMATOVA: Are there microphones in this dimension? I hope not.

> LILLI *takes the glass from her.*

LILLI: You've kept the words alive for all of us.

AKHMATOVA: For a future that doesn't seem to be listening.

LILLI: Don't. You said it yourself: 'They want us to die while we're still alive'.

AKHMATOVA: Not a problem for you these days.

LILLI: Don't give up. Find someone!

AKHMATOVA: What's one woman in a holocaust anyway?

LILLI: You're asking me? It was my life.

AKHMATOVA: Sometimes the gods changed humans into things, leaving consciousness intact. Is that my fate?—to outlive everyone? Old and blind and deaf? I can't survive alone.

LILLI: You will, Anna.

AKHMATOVA: I miss you, Lilli. I can't write without you.

LILLI: Yes, you can.

AKHMATOVA: How?

LILLI: I can't tell you that.

Helen Morse (left) as Lilli Kalinovskaya and Julia Blake as Anna Akhmatova in the 1998 Melbourne Theatre Company production. (Photo: Jeff Busby)

She goes. AKHMATOVA *calls after her:*

AKHMATOVA: What's the point of dying, Lilli, if you don't learn all the answers?!

She becomes aware of RACHEL. RACHEL *walks forward into* AKHMATOVA*'s world.* AKHMATOVA *watches as she examines the room. She finds the teaset, becoming entranced by it.*

From Tsarskoye Selo—the Tsar's village, one of the most beautiful places in the world. My family lived there until I was sixteen. I was born the same year as Charlie Chaplin, the Eiffel Tower and T.S. Eliot. I don't suppose you've heard of any of them, have you?

RACHEL *regards her blankly. She is still holding a cup.*

Take it, why don't you? Show me whose side you're really on.

RACHEL *replaces the cup and puts her hands behind her back. They stare at each other.* AKHMATOVA *retrieves her glass. She looks up at the moon.*

I believed my poetry came from the moon: not a gift from God, a gift from the moon. Perhaps all poets do. I was never loved as a woman of flesh and blood. I was loved as a moon-girl or a mermaid—

She stares, astonished as:

RACHEL: [*the young* AKHMATOVA] Kolya called me his 'moon-girl'. He painted the walls of his room blue, like the sea, with a mermaid swimming there; then we married and the tide went out and I was left on the shore alone. He thought for two poets to be married was ridiculous. Shileyko burned my poems in the samovar. He didn't want a child with me, and he didn't want my poems either. He breathed with the sun—

AKHMATOVA: —and I breathed with the moon. Nikolay flirted with other women and I scarcely wrote at all for years. [*Staring at* RACHEL] Why have I been left alive? What am I meant to do?

The lights begin to fade. The moon and stars disappear. AKHMATOVA *remains.*

SCENE FIVE

RACHEL *and* MIZ *in* MIZ's *room.*

RACHEL: You wanted to see me?

MIZ: Your Eigenface analysis—

RACHEL: Is there a problem?

MIZ: You haven't smiled in three days. Can you explain it?

RACHEL: I suppose I forgot.

MIZ: You forgot? You've been absent from group activities. We've hardly seen you. What have you been doing?

RACHEL: When I'm not with my client I've been in my room. My virtual room. There's a moon there—huge, like it used to be—and stars. I can't really describe what it's like in there, but it's wonderful —

> *She sees that* MIZ *is regarding her coldly, unimpressed.*

Miz, what happens when I leave this job?

MIZ: Surely you've thought about that?

RACHEL: Everyone tries to think it will never happen to them.

MIZ: Oh, it will happen.

RACHEL: We slide further and further down the food chain, servicing lower and lower ranks?

MIZ: None of my concern.

RACHEL: What is your concern?

MIZ: While you're here, you are.

RACHEL: I was put in an isolation chamber because of a ractive—

MIZ: Yes, I know about the ractive.

RACHEL: —Miz, I'm sorry—Want to know what I think?

MIZ: Could that be of any interest?

RACHEL: Everything's an isolation chamber—the whole world... a prison.

MIZ: Let me see a genuine smile in the next three days or you're finished here.

> *Blackout.* MIZ *exits.*

SCENE SIX

SANDOR *is seated.* RACHEL *stands behind him massaging his shoulders. He holds the tardigrade.*

RACHEL: What's wrong?

SANDOR: Nothing's wrong.

RACHEL: Did you have a fight with that poet?

SANDOR: What poet?

RACHEL: The one you said was moving in on your specialty.

SANDOR: No.

RACHEL: What then?

SANDOR: I can't talk about it.

RACHEL: Yes you can. That's one of the things I'm here for. So you can talk things out.

SANDOR: Not this.

RACHEL: Why not?

SANDOR: Confidential.

RACHEL: They're the ones I like best.

SANDOR: No one else knows yet—and you mustn't tell anyone because you'd betray my friend in Management who warned me—we're being shut down.

RACHEL: Who?

SANDOR: The poets. We're being de-listed.

RACHEL: Why?

SANDOR: Economics. They want to get rid of the literary archives. A few people like poets still use them, so de-list the poets, then say no one needs the archives.

RACHEL: You can find something else—you were born a high rank.

SANDOR: I'm a poet! I can't just find something else. I'm not the managerial or engineering type. And women get all the service jobs… How would I pass an Eigenface…? [*He presents a grotesquely false smile.*] I'm sitting in a conference listening to people discuss 'The Iliad', knowing 'The Iliad' won't be there next week. Passed down by word of mouth, then into print, then into digital form—and now about to be switched off. Phttt! Gone!

RACHEL: Then do something.

SANDOR: What? There's nothing I can do. It's already been decided.

RACHEL: You're clever. You can think of something. Ask the other poets to help.

SANDOR: I'd put my friend in Management at risk.

RACHEL: There must be something you can do.

SANDOR: [*to himself*] No more Shakespeare... Shelley... Dante... It's impossible... I can't let this happen... [*He turns to her.*] Will you help me?

RACHEL: How?

SANDOR: We'll need to retrieve from the archives—not far in—just from the first level... How much personal storage have you got?

RACHEL: Hardly used.

SANDOR: I'm going to run out of memory space... I can upload from say... Auden to Rilke...

AKHMATOVA *listens, distressed.*

I'll give you a list. Make sure you get all the Shakespeare.

RACHEL: But I don't have access to the archives!

SANDOR: I'll grant you access.

RACHEL: What if we're caught?

AKHMATOVA: [*unheard by them*] Ask the vital question, girl!

SANDOR: It's important.

RACHEL: More than we are?

SANDOR: Words are important. Words can scrape the skin off your soul.

RACHEL: Sandor, if you get caught you'll get a slap on the wrist and they'll send you home. But I'm already in trouble with Miz. If I get caught—

He takes her hands.

SANDOR: You don't have to be frightened of Miz any more: when I leave I'm going to take you with me.

She stares at him astonished. The lights fade. Blackout. RACHEL *and* SANDOR *sleep.*

SCENE SEVEN

AKHMATOVA *broods over* RACHEL.

AKHMATOVA: Father didn't want us to write poetry. And so, we pretended we didn't. We played on the seashore. We hid our clothes and swam far out to sea at night. A monk asked us what we were doing. We had no idea we were happy. We read Pushkin and what it was like to be persecuted for one's art. Pushkin, who said, 'Go where your secret dreams lead you'. When we grew up we stood with other women outside the prisons. We saw their faces grow old as they waited for news of sons or husbands. When one of them asked us, 'Can you describe this?' we said, 'Yes, I can'. We knew there was a secret writing that inscribed the world, a kind of invisible ink of the universe. And this was poetry. And we knew that it belonged to everyone. And so we began to write for everyone. It was personal, but it spoke of everyone who lived and breathed.

In RACHEL*'s dream* AKHMATOVA *sets a book before her: a large, old-fashioned book resembling a nineteenth-century Bible.* RACHEL *opens it. Inside is a cavity with a smaller book encased in gold. She lifts it out and opens it:*

'Mountains bow before this sorrow.'

AKHMATOVA *waits.*

If I'm waking the dead, forgive me.

RACHEL *studies the book. Lighting change.*

SCENE EIGHT

SANDOR *wakes.*

RACHEL: Why aren't there any women in your list?
AKHMATOVA: Good girl.
SANDOR: Women poets? I've never seen any.
RACHEL: Could there be any?
SANDOR: I doubt it.
RACHEL: I dreamed of a book written by a woman. Perhaps they exist?
SANDOR: Once upon a time, maybe—pre-digitisation.
RACHEL: Not now?

SANDOR: Many books never got transcribed; libraries couldn't afford to scan everything, unless it was science or economics. And many of those that were transcribed have probably been dropped from the indexes.

RACHEL: Why?

SANDOR: It's a hierarchical system: information people hardly ever access gets moved from the first level into the deep archives. Makes it unlikely anyone's going to know to look for it.

RACHEL: But they might still exist?

SANDOR: There are billions of terabytes of data that haven't been accessed in no one knows how long.

RACHEL: So they could be there, somewhere in the deep archives?

SANDOR: It's too dangerous. You could trigger an alert.

RACHEL: Why aren't we allowed to look for them?

SANDOR: The authorities say history stirs things up.

RACHEL: So they fade from memory, like a dream. Dreams that belong to everyone, then they're gone.

SANDOR: Rachel, even if they did exist and you could find them—what would you understand?

The light fades. They exit.

AKHMATOVA: [*distressed*] We're truly in the wood of forgetting.

Blackout. The sound of chimes.

SCENE NINE

TUSYA *enters. The light is dim. She searches anxiously for* AKHMATOVA.

TUSYA: Anna Andreyevna!

She finds AKHMATOVA *in the armchair.*

It's freezing in here!

She rubs AKHMATOVA*'s frozen hands.* AKHMATOVA *opens her eyes.*

AKHMATOVA: Leave me—

TUSYA: [*in an urgent whisper*] Get up!

She tries to help AKHMATOVA *up. She resists.*

AKHMATOVA: No… I'm so tired…

TUSYA: Yes, you were so exhausted with your… with your cleaning you forgot to go to the window! [*Hissing*] Come on, Anna Andreyevna!

AKHMATOVA: I can't…

TUSYA: Yes, you can!

> *She forces* AKHMATOVA *to her feet.*

If I had to stand in a window twice a day, there'd be times when I'd forget too!

> *Slowly she guides* AKHMATOVA *forward to the window.* AKHMATOVA *stands, swaying.*

SCENE TEN

Lights play across MIZ*'s face as she consults a computer.* TUSYA *helps* AKHMATOVA *to her chair and exits. The* AUDITOR *enters.*

MIZ: Can I help you, Auditor?

AUDITOR: What are you doing, and why?

MIZ: I'm checking an Eigenface analysis.

AUDITOR: You haven't been accessing the literary archives?

MIZ: No, why would I do that?

AUDITOR: Your visiting poets are about to be de-listed—

MIZ: No one told me.

AUDITOR: It's not official yet, but someone's been trawling through the literary archives and copying them somewhere else.

MIZ: Why would I care?

AUDITOR: Access was made from this area.

MIZ: Other people use this area. Rachel was here this morning.

AUDITOR: Rachel Sekerov? Why would Rachel be interested? Do you give your girls access to the archives?

MIZ: No! I would never…

AUDITOR: Then how would Rachel gain access? Why would she want to?

MIZ: Why does Rachel do anything these days? Team activity is down, her attitude rating has fallen, unprofessional emotions have been recorded—that's why I'm checking her Eigenface—I suspect she's no longer viable.

AUDITOR: You're intending to log that?

MIZ: Of course.

AUDITOR: It might be wise to reconsider.

MIZ: Why? I'm simply doing my job.

AUDITOR: Is it your job to upload material from archives that are being de-listed?

MIZ: I've told you I wasn't in the archives!

AUDITOR: You've also told me your girls don't have access to the archives. But you do. Your activity may be connected to a leak. Do you have friends on the Board?

MIZ: No. No friends on the Board! [*Covering her ears*] Why are you accusing me of this?

AUDITOR: Perhaps I don't like your face.

MIZ: I've done a lot of work on my face. It's a good face!

AUDITOR: Your misfortune.

MIZ: This is about Rachel! It's because I was going to log her! I wasn't in the archives!

AUDITOR: Probably not, but you'll do. [*He starts to go, then turns.*] Report to my security centre.

He exits. MIZ *follows.*

SCENE ELEVEN

RACHEL *and* SANDOR. *He takes hold of her, shaking her.*

SANDOR: Are you trying to get us killed?

RACHEL: I got everything you asked for!

SANDOR: But you didn't stop!

RACHEL: You said stars are maps—

SANDOR: You didn't stop!

RACHEL: Words are maps!

SANDOR: You went to the deep archives!

RACHEL: Words are important. You said so yourself. There were other people who felt what I feel—

SANDOR: It was an acceptable risk at the first level—

RACHEL: —Life doesn't start and end with me any more. I'm not suspended in a vacuum—

SANDOR: You can forget about history—and if there's a future it's just like now; I hope it was worth it. You've destroyed everything we tried to save.

RACHEL: But I found it.

SANDOR: What?

RACHEL: The poem that scrapes the skin off my soul.

SANDOR: But did you understand it?

RACHEL: Night and stars—a bright moon turning silver—shadows on walls—reflections in water—the dreams of the dead in mirrors—burnt pages—people whispering—

SANDOR: Did you understand?

RACHEL: —a place beyond help—an execution drum—faces streaked with blood—

SANDOR: DID YOU?

RACHEL: No! I didn't! It seemed to be about everything in the world! There were words… feelings—happiness and love and boredom and anger and fear. It was impossible! But it made me feel! It made me think I could write. [*Near tears*] Stupid…

SANDOR: You're not a poet.

RACHEL: Are you?

He stares at her in silence.

SANDOR: Write about what?

RACHEL: The day my tracer went random and I was lost and that girl who looked like me opened the door… Maren, I'd write about Maren… I'd write about Miz… the sky… the moon rising in my virtual room—

SANDOR: Who's going to read them? The only 'literature' people are interested in is spin-offs from games.

RACHEL: Because that's all we were ever given!

SANDOR: What does it matter if the words don't survive? Who's going to care?

RACHEL: I thought you did!

SANDOR: You might as well have jumped up and down and waved your arms in the air and shouted, 'Arrest me!' I could have taken you with me—out of here.

He leaves. RACHEL *remains. Slowly she becomes aware as:*

SCENE TWELVE

TUSYA *forces* AKHMATOVA *to take some tea.*

TUSYA: It's hot. It's good for you. I know you don't want to talk to me.

> AKHMATOVA *looks sharply at her, giving* TUSYA *her full attention for the first time.*

AKHMATOVA: Why wouldn't I want to talk to you?

TUSYA: I'm sorry for the things I said. More than that—until they took Yuri, I was informing on you.

AKHMATOVA: Of course you were.

> TUSYA *stares.*

I've been spied upon for thirty years. I have a nose for it now.

TUSYA: I'm so sorry…

AKHMATOVA: We've all drunk from the bottle marked poison. It disagrees with all of us sooner or later.

TUSYA: Yuri was never safe. You're not supposed to care. Rivers are radioactive, wildlife is dying, people are sick. The land was holy and he was killing it; that's what he said—that it would die because of people like him.

AKHMATOVA: You've been to the prison?

TUSYA: Every day.

AKHMATOVA: Have you managed to speak to anyone? What did they tell you?

TUSYA: 'Ten years without right of correspondence'. We were childhood sweethearts. We waited years—I can wait now.

AKHMATOVA: You don't know what it means, do you, child?

TUSYA: Waiting? Not the way you do.

AKHMATOVA: 'Ten years without right of correspondence': it means 'the highest measure'. It means Yuri is already dead.

> *A silence.*

TUSYA: When they first brought me in for questioning they asked if you and Lilli were ghosts. I wanted to say, 'Yes—that's what we all are—ghosts'. When I walk in the street now no one looks at me. No one speaks. People turn away and avoid my eyes.

AKHMATOVA: You have the leper's rattle in your hand now, as I do.

TUSYA: But I'm not strong like you. I won't survive alone.

AKHMATOVA: You will, Tusya.

TUSYA: Not to know what happened—that's the hard part. So much is missing from our lives. I teach history, and I don't know what the real history is. Sometimes I think it's all a giant hallucination. And it's sad... it makes me angry... not to know how people suffered, and how they gave each other strength.

> AKHMATOVA *begins to write.* RACHEL *draws near, speaking the words aloud:*

RACHEL: Everything is looted, bartered, betrayed,
            The black wing of death is hovering,
            And anguish gnaws through our bones—
Why then is there such a radiance?
            The incomparable forest near the town
            Holds the scent of cherry trees,
            At night new constellations appear in the sky.

            And the miraculous is drawing closer,
            Unknown to any of us,
            Yet longed for from the beginning of time.

> AKHMATOVA *hands the poem to* TUSYA. TUSYA *begins to memorise it.*

SCENE THIRTEEN

SANDOR *enters and puts his arms around* RACHEL.

RACHEL: I'm sorry, Sandor. What will they do to us? Will they let us be together?

SANDOR: You're here to serve me; say I ordered you.

RACHEL: I feel as if I've never been awake before.

SANDOR: I wanted to give you the real sky.

RACHEL: Awake for a blink of time, and then asleep. I don't feel less, now that I know I am less. I know what we once were.

The AUDITOR *enters.* SANDOR *pushes* RACHEL *away.*

SANDOR: Tell your superiors I was pleased with your work.

RACHEL *hesitates.*

Go, Rachel.

AUDITOR: Stay.

She stops, frightened. He turns to SANDOR.

Is there something you'd like to tell me, Sandor Voss?

SANDOR: No.

AUDITOR: Unauthorised use of the deep archives is a capital offence. Your friend admitted the leak.

SANDOR: What friend?

AUDITOR: Everyone confesses, Sandor. So will you. Why couldn't you be satisfied with the first level? You might have gotten away with that, but the deep archives? You signed your own death warrant.

SANDOR: Leave, Rachel—

RACHEL: The deep archives were my idea!

SANDOR: Rachel can barely read!

AUDITOR: [*looking from one to the other*] Foolish. There are no dramas in real life—no love, no passion. Why create dissatisfaction and disorder? The horizon you see is the only horizon.

RACHEL: It was my fault—not his!

AUDITOR: We know who helped him. Your Miz confessed.

RACHEL: Miz? What do you mean, Miz? This is nothing to do with her.

TUSYA *hands* AKHMATOVA *back the poem.*

TUSYA: [*to* AKHMATOVA] They say the human body isn't worth much. Suddenly mine feels immensely more valuable.

AKHMATOVA: [*softly*] Be sure, Tusya.

SANDOR: [*to* AUDITOR] You took too long, Auditor.

AUDITOR: You're here, aren't you?

SANDOR: Too late for you.

AKHMATOVA *tears the page from the notebook.*

AKHMATOVA: [*looking at* TUSYA] You're sure?

TUSYA: I'm sure.

AKHMATOVA *lights a match and holds the poem to the flame.*

SANDOR: [*to* AUDITOR, *as the poem burns*] Think of a stream of binary data—hiding anywhere, lying dormant for a hundred years if necessary. But when it comes to life, it multiplies itself exponentially in days. It's indestructible. [*He smiles at* RACHEL.] I got the idea from a little bear.

AUDITOR: [*realising*] You've created a virus.

SANDOR: Maybe years from now you'll receive a message in your in-box... 'Sailing to Byzantium'... or 'The Song of Solomon'... [*looking at* RACHEL] ... maybe something by a woman. It's how 'Tardigrade' replicates: an individual copy randomly sending a random poem to a random recipient. If only one person in a thousand responds it'll continue to spread, faster than the authorities can look for it. Even if you find one copy of the program, you'll never find them all.

AUDITOR: You released it?

SANDOR: It's done.

AUDITOR: Undo it!

SANDOR: I can't. It's indestructible.

AUDITOR: Prisoner Voss, you are to report to my security centre for auditing.

SANDOR: Interesting word, 'audit'... It once referred to books, not people—

AUDITOR: You can forget the words. Everyone else has.

The AUDITOR *steps back, gesturing to* SANDOR *to precede him.*

Mr Voss?

RACHEL *runs to* SANDOR *and throws her arms around him.* SANDOR *hugs her hard. The* AUDITOR *crosses to intervene.* RACHEL *refuses to let go.* SANDOR *pushes her from him and exits, the* AUDITOR *following.* RACHEL *remains. Blackout.* AKHMATOVA *and* TUSYA *exit.*

SCENE FOURTEEN

RACHEL *consults her computer. Lights play across her face as she listens absorbed.*

RACHEL: Freedom—

'ELIZA': [*voice-over, warm, comforting*] Ease of movement or action. Exemption from external control.

RACHEL: Flute—

'ELIZA': [*voice-over*] A musical wind instrument consisting of a tube with a series of finger holes or keys.

RACHEL: Veil—

'ELIZA': [*voice-over*] A piece of material worn over the head or face. Something that covers, screens or conceals.

RACHEL: Dante—

'ELIZA': [*voice-over, correcting her pronunciation*] Dante. Dante Alighieri, 1265 to 1321. Italian poet.

RACHEL: Inferno—

'ELIZA': [*voice-over*] Hell.

SCENE FIFTEEN

The lights begin to fade. AKHMATOVA *comes downstage. Quietly, to herself:*

AKHMATOVA: At night I wait for her,
       Sometimes with life hanging by a thread…
       What do fame or freedom or even youth matter?
       She is my beloved guest, flute in hand.

       She comes to me, pushing aside her veil,
       And looks at me attentively as I ask her:
       'Were you Dante's guide when he wrote the Inferno?'
       'Yes,' she says, 'I was'.

The lights fade.

THE END